I0760014

VEGAN ASIAN STREET FOOD

YANG LiU

VEGAN ASIAN STREET FOOD

YANG LIU

PHOTOGRAPHS BY KATHARINA PINCZOLITS

Hardie Grant

BOOKS

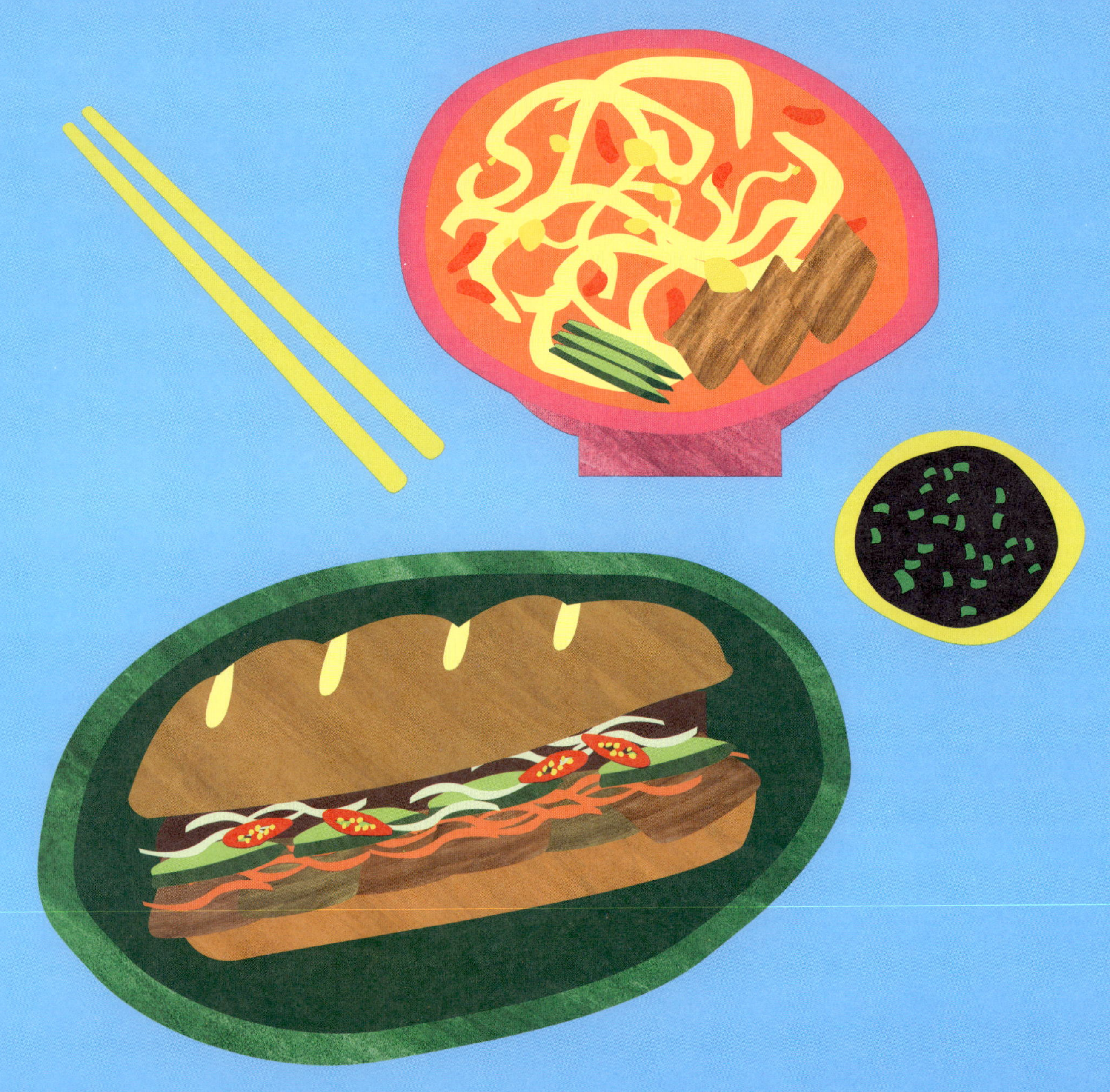

INTRODUCTION

Asian street food transports you into the heart of a place's culture with a sensory explosion. Whether it's the markets of Bangkok or the narrow laneways of Shanghai, the streets are the liveliest part of an Asian city. It is where the locals meet after school or work when they want a quick, tasty meal; where friends get together to chat and eat; and where tourists can find authentic and affordable culinary experiences, and get a glimpse into local life.

Street food is fast, hot, endlessly creative and full of personality – a vivid reflection of a city and its people. For many street vendors, their food represents a craft that has been passed down for generations. They might sell only one or two different items, made with techniques perfected over years.

In many Asian countries, street food isn't just a quick snack; it's an integral part of everyday life. Food stalls are open long hours and vendors build a connection with the local residents. It is common for generations of the same family to keep going back to the same vendors, who become a part of their lives and memories.

Traditionally, many street food dishes contain meat or fish. But almost all of them can be made vegan – and delicious – using ingredients such as mushrooms, tofu and plant-based mince.

Another feature of Asian street food is its sustainability. Many vendors source their ingredients daily from the nearby markets, and their offerings change depending on the season and availability. They also make the most of limited resources by using every possible part of an ingredient. Packaging is minimised, especially in tropical areas, where street food can be wrapped in banana leaves or other parts of plants. For example, in some Southeast Asian countries and in China, you can find vegan coconut-based street foods that use all parts of the coconut, such as sticky rice that is mixed with the juice and the flesh, then steamed and served in the coconut shell. In today's world, these practices are more relevant than ever.

During my early childhood in Hunan, I lived with my grandmother, my cousins and my aunt. The perfect summer day started with rice noodles for breakfast. In general, the type of street food we ate depended on the season, but the one thing we always had, regardless of the time of year, was spicy rice noodles. At the end of the street we lived on, there was an elderly rice noodle vendor whose noodles were so good that they were always sold out by 9 am. My cousins and I would get up extra early just to make sure we didn't miss out.

MY STORY WITH STREET FOOD

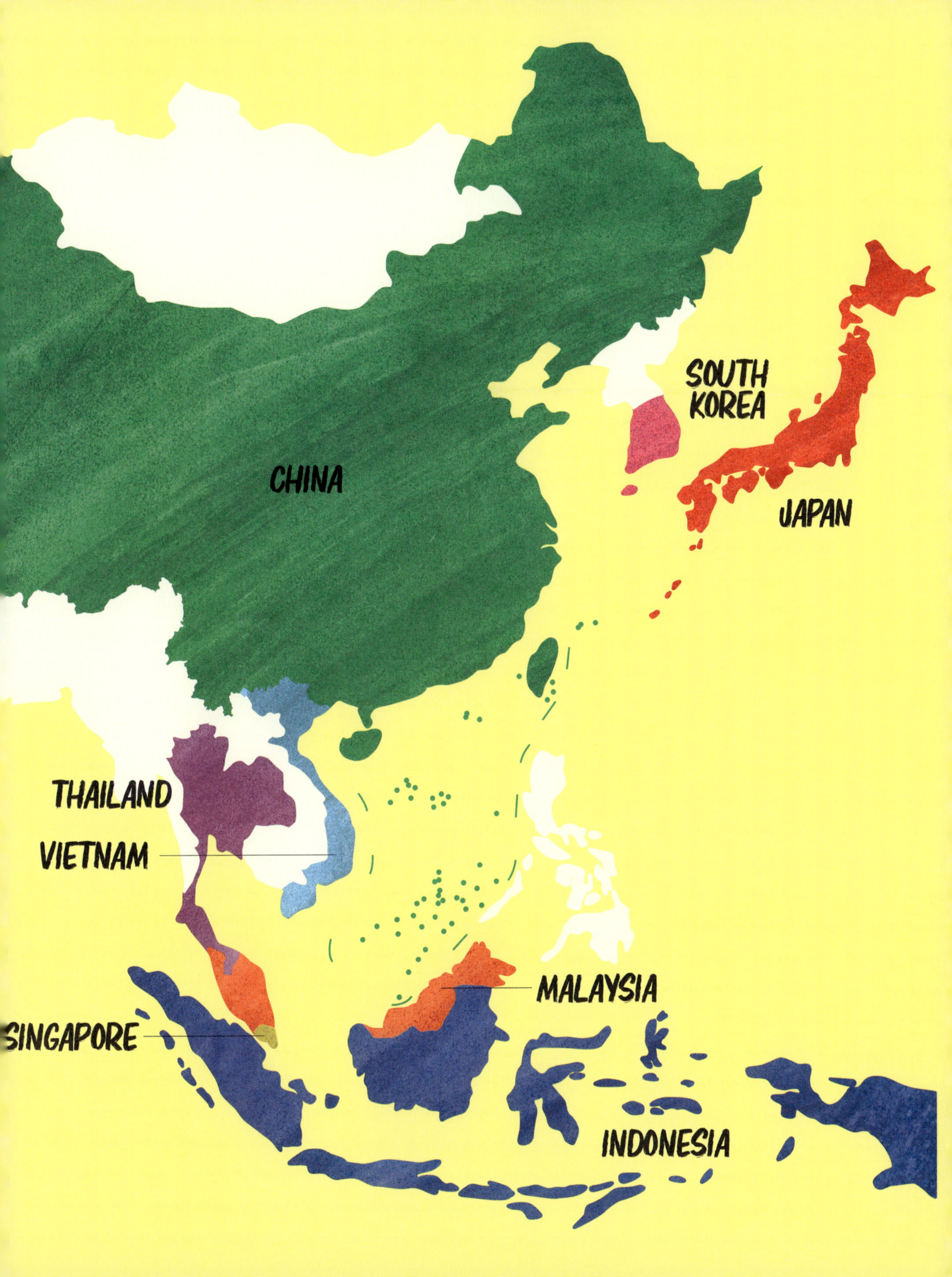

SOUTH KOREA
CHINA
JAPAN
THAILAND
VIETNAM
MALAYSIA
SINGAPORE
INDONESIA

Later in the day, for our afternoon snack, we would go out again for ice jelly, a famous summer dessert in China's southern regions. Traditionally vegan, ice jelly is made from the seeds of the *Nicandra physalodes* plant. In my city, it is served with brown sugar water. A similar dessert, bingfen (page 73), originated in Sichuan and has gained popularity in recent years as a trendy street food across China. Unlike the simpler ice jelly, bingfen is often topped with a wide variety of ingredients, including fresh fruits, raisins, peanuts, red (adzuki) beans and dried hawthorn slices.

After having dinner at home, I often played Chinese chequers with my cousins. Around 9 or 10 pm, we would go out once more, for a second dinner. There were many stands that only opened at night, and my aunt would buy us street barbecue, followed by ice cream or shaved ice. The shaved ice, which was handmade, came in many different shapes – my favourite was a little bear holding up a tiny bamboo umbrella. Afterwards, we would walk along the river, not returning home until after midnight.

In winter, when it gets very cold in Hunan, we would buy roasted sweet potatoes and chestnuts from the street vendors. We'd cradle the potatoes, which were roasted whole, to warm up our hands. Even now when I eat roasted sweet potatoes, I can smell the humid winter air and visualise my cousins and I sitting around the coal stove together.

Unlike today, when many street foods are available across the country, in the 1990s and early 2000s, many regional specialities were only available in or near their place of origin. When I moved in with my mother in Guangzhou aged six, I really missed the food I'd grown to love during my early childhood in Hunan. But I soon grew to love the Cantonese street food, which was much less spicy and quite different.

On my walk to primary school, I would queue up at a breakfast stand to buy pan-fried dumplings filled with garlic chives. And during lunch breaks, I would cross the street to a back alley where there were two food stalls: one selling Cantonese stir-fried hor fun (flat rice noodles) and another selling jyu cheung fun (rice-noodle rolls, page 46), both of which I love. I would stand in front of the fried-noodle stall, completely fascinated by the cooking process: how the noodles were tossed on a hot flat griddle, how the different soy sauces were squeezed out of the bottle and almost immediately caramelised, how the ingredients were turned and mixed with two flat spatulas. The whole process was so smooth and practised.

When I met up with friends, food was always involved. We often went to commercial streets where there were many food stalls, or to night markets and small eateries. We were excited to discover new spots and good street food. We didn't have much pocket money, but we would each buy an item and share.

During high school, I was at school from 8 am to 9 pm every day except Sunday. (On Saturdays, we were allowed to leave a little earlier.) The food at the school canteen was horrible, so we would always go out for lunch and dinner. Often, the whole class would order bubble tea together, because for every five drinks, we would get one free. There are almost always food stalls dotted around schools during lunch and dinner breaks, offering all kinds of food options for hungry students.

My university days were even more closely connected with street food, as I had more time and a bit more money to spare. I went to university on a huge island in the Pearl River, where there are ten universities and multiple villages. At that time, there were hardly any restaurants on the island, which is quite a long way from the city centre, but the street food options were limitless. Students would go out around midnight for late-night snacks and the vendors were open until 3 or 4 am. My friends and I would walk, cycle and ferry all over the island to try different foods. I remember cycling for an hour one day just to try the clay pot rice sold at a particular roadside eatery; it was the best clay pot rice I have eaten to this day.

Later, after becoming vegan, I travelled through Asia and fell in love with street foods from different countries. This is when I realised that the most authentic food of a cuisine can be found at its street markets. These food explorations have opened my eyes to culinary and cultural experiences beyond China. I have discovered many delicious dishes from many different countries, inspiring me to write this cookbook, through which I hope I can pass my love of Asian street food on to you.

TIPS ON HOW TO USE THIS BOOK

INGREDIENTS

The coconut cream that is used in many recipes refers to the canned product that has a consistency thicker than milk and is commonly used for cooking, rather than the thinner coconut milk that also comes in a tin or bottle and may be used for drinking.

Many recipes use fresh chillies. I never remove the seeds when I'm cooking; however, you can do so if you want less heat in the dish.

My preferred tofu for cooking is tender (or semi-firm) tofu, which is firmer than silken tofu but softer and more easily breakable than firm tofu. It has a smooth texture and a mild flavour.

When a recipe calls for sugar and I haven't specified a type, either a light-brown cane sugar (soft brown sugar) or white granulated sugar will work. Some recipes call for coconut (palm) sugar; made from the sap of the flower of the coconut palm, this is the sugar typically used in Thailand. Usually sold in blocks or in grated form, it is labelled either 'palm sugar' or 'coconut sugar'. Ensure that you use this type rather than jaggery, which is also called palm sugar but contains more cane sugar.

The amount of oil in the recipes is simply a guide; how much you need will depend on your cooking equipment. If you have a non-stick wok or pan, you'll need less oil than if you use a different type.

Canola (rapeseed), corn (maize), peanut or soybean oil can be used as the cooking oil in all the recipes. All these oils have a high smoking point, which is essential for the stir-frying, pan-frying and deep-frying that is common in Asian cuisines. Avoid using oils that have a particularly low smoking point, such as extra-virgin olive oil or linseed oil. When these oils smoke, they become unstable and create harmful chemicals.

As for the measurements, you can adjust them a little to your taste and in accordance with the products you use. For example, different brands of sauce, including soy sauce, vary in taste and saltiness.

MEASUREMENTS AND COOKING TIMES

All cooking times given are approximate. The exact cooking time will differ depending on the type of stove, how strong the heat is and which cooking utensils you use. It is much more important to observe the state of the ingredients rather than to work to a timer. For example, I normally stir-fry chopped garlic for 30 seconds before adding other ingredients, but if you have a very strong flame and the garlic is turning golden after 20 seconds, the next ingredient should be added at this point. Or if your flame is weak and the garlic only becomes fragrant after 1 minute, then the cooking time should be increased slightly for each step in the method.

The recipes in this book were cooked in a fan-forced or convection oven. If using a conventional oven, increase the temperature by 20°C (70°F).

The tablespoons used are 15 ml (½ fl oz); cooks using 20 ml (¾ fl oz) tablespoons should be scant with their tablespoon measurements. Metric cup measurements are used, with 250 ml (8½ fl oz) being 1 cup; in the US, a cup is just smaller, at 240 ml (8 fl oz), so American cooks should be generous in their cup measurements.

The number of serves that each recipe yields are for reference only.

PRODUCT RECOMMENDATIONS

For a comprehensive list of sauces and other products available in supermarkets or Asian stores, visit my website: littlericenoodle.com/vegan-streetfood-condiments.

雨光
โจ๊ก - ข้าวหน้าไก่

THT
แปลงนาม หูฉลามรังนก
義福巷魚翅燕窩
SHARK'S FIN & BIRD'S NES

Throughout this book, you'll find many condiments and ingredients commonly used in either just one cuisine or across multiple cuisines. This chapter provides recipes for some of the ingredients that are more difficult to find, especially those that are not originally vegan, such as fish sauce and condensed milk. For more information on other commonly used basic ingredients, such as sweet soy sauce (kecap manis), Thai black soy sauce, Golden Mountain seasoning sauce and others, visit littlericenoodle.com.

ESSENTIAL INGREDIENTS

PREPARATION TIME
1 hour

COOKING TIME
10 minutes

MAKES
400 ml (13½ fl oz)

Fish sauce is one of the essential condiments in Southeast Asian cooking, and it's not always easy to find a vegan substitute. This simple recipe, with only five ingredients, enables you to make your own vegan 'fish' sauce at home. The soy sauce and vegan oyster sauce give it a good savoury flavour, the shiitake and kelp provide the fish-like element, and the yeast extract paste gives it an extra umami boost.

VEGAN FISH SAUCE

- 5 dried shiitake mushrooms
- 1 kelp sheet about 10 × 15 cm (4 × 6 in)
- 2 tablespoons soy sauce
- 2 tablespoons vegan oyster sauce
- 2 teaspoons yeast extract paste (for example, Vegemite or Marmite)

Combine the shiitake, kelp and 600 ml (20½ fl oz) of water in a large pot and soak for 1 hour.

Place the pot over low–medium heat, bring to a simmer and cook for 10 minutes.

Take the kelp and shiitake out and discard. Turn off the heat and stir in soy sauce, vegan oyster sauce and yeast extract paste.

Set aside to cool then transfer to an airtight container and store in the fridge for up to 2 weeks.

NƯỚC CHẤM (VIETNAMESE DIPPING SAUCE)

PREPARATION TIME
10 minutes

MAKES
200 ml (7 fl oz)

Nước chấm is a classic Vietnamese dipping sauce with the perfect balance of spiciness, sourness, sweetness and saltiness. It is typically served with chả giò/nem rán (spring rolls) and gỏi cuốn (summer rolls) for dipping, or used as a dressing for cold vermicelli dishes such as bún thịt nướng chả giò (rice vermicelli with vegan grilled 'meat'). Simple to make with just a few key ingredients, this dish is best enjoyed as fresh as possible, so I recommend making it in small portions and using it immediately rather than making a large batch.

- 5 garlic cloves, finely chopped
- 4 birdseye chillies, destemmed and finely chopped
- 2 teaspoons coconut (palm) sugar
- 100 ml (3½ fl oz) freshly squeezed lime juice
- 3 tablespoons Vegan fish sauce (page 18)

Combine all the ingredients with 60 ml (2 fl oz/¼ cup) of water and set aside for 10 minutes to allow the flavours to develop.

Transfer to an airtight container and store in the fridge. It is best to consume the sauce within 48 hours.

PREPARATION TIME
5 minutes

COOKING TIME
20 minutes

MAKES
500 ml (17 fl oz/2 cups)

This famous chilli oil recipe from Sichuan is very versatile, rich and aromatic with minimal spicy heat. The method is simple, but the finished oil makes the best base seasoning for many recipes, especially cold dishes such as noodles and salads. It's also great as a dip for dumplings and bao'zi (steamed bao buns). You can use canola (rapeseed) or corn (maize) oil, but avoid using oils with a low smoking point, such as olive oil.

Sand ginger slices can be bought in dried form from Asian stores. The spice has a strong aroma and a peppery flavour that adds depth to many Southeast Asian dishes.

油泼辣子
YOU PO LA ZI (CHILLI OIL)

- 100 g (3½ oz) chilli flakes
- 30 g (1 oz) toasted white sesame seeds
- 50 g (1¾ oz) fresh ginger
- 1 cinnamon stick
- 3 star anise
- 1 tsaoko pod (Chinese black cardamom)
- 5 g (⅛ oz) sand ginger slices
- 5 dried bay leaves
- 1 tablespoon cloves
- 1 tablespoon whole sichuan peppercorns
- 500 ml (17 fl oz/2 cups) canola (rapeseed) oil or corn (maize) oil
- 1 small onion, quartered
- 80 g (2¾ oz) leek (white part only), cut into large chunks
- ½ teaspoon thirteen-spice

Combine the chilli flakes and sesame seeds in a large bowl and set aside. Smack the fresh ginger a bit with the flat edge of a knife to crush it a little, then slice it. Briefly rinse the dried whole spices separately (cinnamon stick, star anise, tsaoko, sand ginger, bay leaves, cloves and peppercorns) with water so they don't burn when cooked.

Heat the oil in a saucepan over low–medium heat. Fry the onion, leek, fresh ginger, cinnamon stick, star anise, tsaoko and sand ginger for about 10 minutes. Add the bay leaves and fry for 2 minutes more. Add the cloves and sichuan peppercorns and fry, stirring, for another 3 minutes. When the oil reaches 160–170°C (320–340°F) – you can tell it's hot enough when lots of tiny bubbles immediately form around a wooden chopstick placed into the oil – carefully strain the hot oil through a fine-mesh sieve into a clean saucepan or heatproof jug, discarding solids.

Pour half of the hot oil slowly over the chilli flakes and sesame. Stir well, then wait 30 seconds before pouring in the remaining hot oil. Stir again, then add the thirteen-spice and mix well.

Allow to cool completely before pouring into a sterilised jar. The oil will keep for up to 3 months when stored in a cool, dark place. Just make sure you use a clean spoon every time to avoid contaminating the oil.

PREPARATION TIME
10 minutes

COOKING TIME
20 minutes

MAKES
400 g (14 oz)

A chilli paste used throughout Malaysian, Singaporean and Indonesian cuisine, sambal comes in many varieties. Sambal oelek is the most common, made with fresh chilli, vinegar and salt. Sambal mangga is another well-known Indonesian sambal, made with unripe mango for a distinct, refreshing taste. Another is sambal nanas, which includes pineapple to create a balance of sour, sweet and spicy flavours.

This simple vegan version uses fermented soy bean paste (I buy the brand Healthy Boy) instead of the more traditional shrimp paste and can be used in many dishes, including the Malaysian rice dish nasi lemak.

SAMBAL (SPICY CHILLI PASTE)

- 30 g (1 oz) dried chilli, soaked in hot water for 15 minutes, then drained
- 100 g (3½ oz) fresh cayenne chillies, destemmed and roughly chopped
- 6 garlic cloves
- 60 g (2 oz) red onion, roughly chopped
- 120 g (4½ oz) shallots, roughly chopped
- 1 tablespoon soy bean paste
- 1 lemongrass stalk (white part only), sliced
- 100 ml (3½ fl oz) canola (rapeseed) oil
- 2 tablespoons coconut (palm) sugar
- 2 tablespoons tamarind sauce
- 1 teaspoon salt

Combine soaked chillies, cayenne chilli, garlic, red onion, shallot, soy bean paste, lemongrass, oil and 80 ml (2½ fl oz/⅓ cup) of water in a food processor or blender and mix on high speed until a coarse paste forms. If you prefer a smoother sambal, mix it a little longer.

Cook the sambal in a saucepan over low–medium heat, stirring, for 15–20 minutes until it turns dark red and the texture thickens. Add the sugar, tamarind sauce and salt, stir for another minute then turn off the heat.

Store in a sterilised jar in the fridge for up to 1 month. Be sure to use a clean spoon when scooping it out to avoid contaminating the paste.

PREPARATION TIME
10 minutes

COOKING TIME
20 minutes

MAKES
700 g (1 lb 9 oz)

Saté is the Indonesian word for grilled meat skewers, which are typically served with the peanutty saus saté. A staple in traditional Indonesian cuisine, it's a famous street food in many Southeast Asian countries, such as Malaysia, Singapore and Thailand (where it is more familiarly spelt 'satay').

With a similar base to sambal, saus saté is used to add depth and flavour to many dishes, such as stir-fries, noodles and rice dishes. It's also delicious as a dipping sauce for grilled or fried foods, or as a dressing for salads such as gado-gado.

SAUS SATÉ (SATAY SAUCE)

- 6 garlic cloves
- 3 shallots, sliced
- 1 lemongrass stalk, sliced
- 30 g (1 oz) galangal, sliced
- 20 g (¾ oz) dried chillies, soaked in hot water for 15 minutes, then drained
- 180 ml (6 fl oz/¾ cup) canola (rapeseed) oil
- 40 g (1½ oz) coconut (palm) sugar
- 1 teaspoon ground coriander
- 1 teaspoon curry powder
- 200 g (7 oz) roasted unsalted peanuts, finely crushed
- 3 tablespoons tamarind sauce
- 2 tablespoons sweet soy sauce (kecap manis)
- salt

Combine the garlic, shallot, lemongrass, galangal, soaked chillies and oil in a blender or food processor and mix until a paste forms.

Cook the paste in a saucepan over low–medium heat for about 10–15 minutes, stirring, until it becomes dense and the oil separates.

Add the sugar, coriander, curry powder and 300 ml (10 fl oz) of water, and stir to dissolve. Bring the mixture to a simmer, then stir in the crushed peanuts. Stir in the tamarind sauce and soy sauce, then reduce heat to low and continue to simmer, stirring, for 3–5 minutes. Season with salt to taste then remove from the heat and set aside to cool.

Store in an airtight container in the fridge for up to 7 days.

PREPARATION TIME
5 minutes

COOKING TIME
1 hour

MAKES
200 ml (7 fl oz)

Condensed milk is a thick, sweet and creamy milk product made by removing most of the water from regular milk and adding sugar. Its smooth texture and rich flavour make it ideal for use in Southeast Asian desserts and drinks. It's used in cha yen (Thai iced tea), in Malaysia's national drink teh tarik (pulled milk tea), and in cà phê sữa đá (Vietnamese iced coffee).

I developed this simple recipe for plant-based condensed milk using coconut cream, which has a strong aroma, a thick texture and a higher amount of fat than other plant-based milk products.

COCONUT CONDENSED MILK

- 400 ml (13½ fl oz) coconut cream
- 80 g (2¾ oz) sugar

Cook the coconut cream and sugar in a saucepan over low heat, stirring occasionally, for about 1 hour, until the volume reduces by half and it has the consistency of condensed milk. Set aside to cool.

Once cooled, store in an airtight container in the fridge for up to 1 week.

CHINA

The history of street food in China can be traced back centuries and varies greatly between regions. The dishes typical to each region strongly reflect the climate, geography and fresh produce of the local area.

Hunan, the region where I was born, is very hilly and humid – boiling hot in summer and extremely cold in winter. According to traditional Chinese medicine, humidity invades the body, especially when it's cold, and creates 'dampness' or an imbalance that can result in health problems such as rheumatism. Hence the spicy local dishes with a warming effect. Sichuan and Chongqing, where the climate is also very humid, are renowned for their hotpot dishes.

The region of Yunnan is famous for its wild mushrooms (it is estimated that more than 40 per cent of the world's edible mushrooms grow here). So, it is unsurprising that wild mushrooms play an essential part in Yunnanese cuisine, in dishes such as crossing-the-bridge rice noodles.

In the northwestern regions, where fresh vegetables and fruits are scarce because of the terrain, street food is very meat-centric. In the regions along the coast, street food is generally seafood-centric.

Some simple street foods, such as suan la fen (page 35) and jianbing guozi (page 36), use common ingredients and are popular across regions. Others are more time-consuming and made using fresh ingredients specific to an area, making them more difficult to replicate. For example, the fundamental ingredient in my hometown's most typical noodle dish is a fresh, local rice noodle that requires a special kind of rice and particular traditional techniques. Without these exact noodles, the dish is soulless. And since fresh rice noodles have to be transported daily from Shaoyang, they can't travel far beyond the borders of Hunan, meaning the dish remains a distinct local speciality.

PREPARATION TIME
15 minutes

COOKING TIME
15 minutes

SERVES
2

Invented in the streets, this is the most famous noodle dish from Sichuan. 'Dan dan' means 'carrying pole' in Chinese, as originally these noodles were sold by vendors walking around the city carrying a pole. One side of the pole held the stove to cook the noodles, while the other side was loaded with all the ingredients.

Traditionally, dan dan noodles are topped with minced pork. For this vegan version, I use vegan mince instead. If your sesame paste is very thick, mix in one or two tablespoons of sesame oil until it reaches a pourable consistency.

担担面
DAN DAN MIAN (DAN DAN NOODLES)

- 2 garlic cloves, finely chopped
- 10 g (¼ oz) fresh ginger, finely chopped
- 300 g (10½ oz) fresh alkaline wheat noodles, or 200 g (7 oz) dried
- 1 tablespoon canola (rapeseed) oil
- 100 g (3½ oz) vegan mince
- ½ teaspoon Chinese five-spice
- 60 ml (2 fl oz/¼ cup) soy sauce
- 2 tablespoons sichuan preserved mustard greens (sui mi ya cai), found at most Asian stores)
- 60 ml (2 fl oz/¼ cup) Chilli oil (page 23)
- 1 tablespoon sesame oil
- 2 tablespoons sesame paste
- ½ teaspoon ground sichuan peppercorns
- 1 teaspoon toasted white sesame seeds
- 50 g (1¾ oz/⅓ cup) roasted salted peanuts, crushed
- 2 spring onions (scallions), sliced

Mix the garlic, ginger and 90 ml (3 fl oz) of water in a bowl, and set aside for about 10 minutes. Strain to remove the garlic and ginger, reserving the water.

Cook the noodles according to the packet instructions until al dente.

Heat a non-stick frying pan over medium heat until hot. Stir-fry the oil and vegan mince for about 3 minutes, breaking up into small pieces with a spatula, until it changes colour and is cooked through. Stir in the five-spice and 1 tablespoon of the soy sauce and transfer the mixture to a bowl.

Return the pan to the heat, add the sichuan preserved mustard greens and stir-fry for about 30 seconds, then transfer to a separate bowl and set aside.

Divide the noodles, remaining soy sauce, the garlic-ginger water, chilli oil, sesame oil, sesame paste, sichuan peppercorns and sesame seeds between two serving bowls.

Divide the vegan mince mixture, preserved mustard greens, crushed peanuts and spring onion between the bowls. Mix everything well before serving.

PREPARATION TIME
2 hours

COOKING TIME
15 minutes

SERVES
2

Hot sour noodles are originally from Chongqing and, in the last two decades, have become one of the most renowned street foods in China. Made from sweet potato starch, these noodles have a distinctive colour and a uniquely chewy, elastic texture that sets them apart from wheat or rice noodles.

As the name suggests, the dish is spicy and sour, with the noodles floating in a hot soup full of flavour. Topped with crunchy fried soybeans and tangy pickled long beans for an extra punch of sourness, it is super appetising and satisfying.

酸辣粉

SUAN LA FEN (HOT SOUR NOODLES)

- 30 g (1 oz) dried soybeans
- 200 g (7 oz) sweet potato noodles
- 100 ml (3½ fl oz) canola (rapeseed) oil
- 90 ml (3 fl oz) Chilli oil (page 23)
- 60 ml (2 fl oz/¼ cup) soy sauce
- 120 ml (4 fl oz) Chinese dark vinegar
- 2 tablespoons sesame oil
- 1 teaspoon Chinese five-spice
- 15 g (½ oz) fresh ginger, finely chopped
- 3 garlic cloves, finely chopped
- 600 ml (20½ fl oz) vegetable stock
- 50 g (1¾ oz) pickled long beans, sliced into short lengths
- 2 spring onions (scallions), sliced
- coriander (cilantro) sprigs, to serve

Soak the soybeans in water for 2 hours, then drain. Soak the sweet potato noodles in lukewarm water for 30 minutes, then drain.

Add the canola oil and soybeans to a small saucepan over low–medium heat. Allow the soybeans to deep-fry for a few minutes while the oil heats up, until they are wrinkly and crispy on the outside. Remove them with a slotted spoon or a sieve and set aside for a minute or so. Return the soybeans to the pan and deep-fry again for 30 seconds. This will make them extra crispy. Remove from the oil and set aside.

Combine the chilli oil, soy sauce, dark vinegar, sesame oil, five-spice, ginger and garlic, then divide the mixture between two serving bowls.

Bring the stock to the boil in a medium saucepan over medium heat. Add the sweet potato noodles and cook according to the packet instructions until they are translucent and al dente, then divide the noodles and the soup between the bowls. Toss to combine with the sauce.

Divide the fried soybeans, pickled long beans, spring onion and coriander between the bowls and serve.

PREPARATION TIME
15 minutes

COOKING TIME
15 minutes

MAKES
2 (diameter 32 cm/12½ in)

Originally from Tianjin, this dish is cooked on a specially designed griddle and resembles a savoury French crepe. It was typically sold by street vendors as a late-night snack but is now mainly eaten for breakfast. 'Jianbing' means 'pan-fried pancake' while 'guozi' refers to the thin, crisp fried dough in the middle, which adds delightful crunch to every bite.

The recipe has evolved over time and throughout regions. This vegan version features a mung bean flour batter and fried wonton wrappers as the crispy filling. Vegan frankfurts (sausages) are usually available at larger local supermarkets.

煎饼果子
JIANBING GUOZI (SAVOURY CREPE)

- ½ teaspoon cornflour (cornstarch)
- 3 tablespoons tianmian sauce (sweet bean sauce, 甜面酱 酱)
- 1 tablespoon soybean paste
- 1 teaspoon sugar
- ½ teaspoon Chinese five-spice
- 100 ml (3½ fl oz) canola (rapeseed) oil, plus extra for greasing
- 8 wonton wrappers
- 130 g (4½ oz) mung bean flour
- 1 tablespoon black sesame seeds
- 2 tablespoons Chilli oil (page 23)
- 2 vegan frankfurts (sausages), cut lengthways
- 4 lettuce leaves
- 30 g (1 oz) spicy pickled radish, chopped
- 2 spring onions (scallions), sliced
- 1 coriander (cilantro) sprig, chopped

Mix 60 ml (2 fl oz/¼ cup) of water and the cornflour in a saucepan over medium heat until the cornflour is hot and dissolved. Add the tianmian sauce and soybean paste, reduce heat to low and cook, stirring, for 1 minute. Mix in the sugar and five-spice, then turn off the heat.

Heat the oil in a small saucepan over medium–high heat. To check whether the oil is hot enough for deep-frying, hold a wooden chopstick in the oil. If it is immediately surrounded by tiny bubbles, the oil is ready to use. Working one at a time, drop the wonton wrappers into the oil and cook until both sides are golden and crispy. Set aside.

Mix the mung bean flour with 180 ml (6 fl oz/ ¾ cup) of water in a large bowl. Heat a non-stick crepe pan over medium heat and brush with a thin layer of extra canola oil. Pour half of the mung bean batter into the pan and use a crepe spreader to spread the batter until it becomes a thin and round layer. Cook for about 3–4 minutes until the batter is cooked and holds its shape.

Sprinkle the jianbing with half a tablespoon of the black sesame seeds, then flip. Spread half the jianbing with 2 tablespoons of the tianmian sauce mixture and 1 tablespoon of the chilli oil. Add 2 pieces of vegan frankfurt in the centre.

When the base of the jianbing starts to crisp, arrange 4 fried wonton wrappers over it. Top with 2 of the lettuce leaves and half of the pickled radish, spring onion and coriander. Fold in half, roll it carefully, flip the wrapped jianbing around then cut it in half to serve. Repeat with remaining ingredients.

PREPARATION TIME
15 minutes

COOKING TIME
15 minutes

MAKES
4

Scallion pancakes are loved for their crispy, flaky layers and savoury flavour. Easy to make, they're the essence of comfort food and are just right for breakfast, lunch or a late-night snack. The dough is rolled out thinly, brushed with oil and sprinkled generously with chopped scallions (spring onions), then folded and rolled again to create multiple layers. Once cooked on a hot griddle, the outside becomes golden and crispy while the inside remains soft and chewy, with the scallions adding extra aroma and taste. They're an example of how basic ingredients can be transformed into something truly delicious.

葱油饼

CONG YOU BING (SCALLION PANCAKES)

- 300 g (10½ oz) plain (all-purpose) wheat flour, plus extra for dusting
- 1 teaspoon salt
- 50 ml (1¾ fl oz) canola (rapeseed) oil
- 6 spring onions (scallions), thinly sliced
- 1 teaspoon Chinese five-spice

Mix the flour with a pinch of salt and 150 ml (5 fl oz) of water and knead to form a dough. Put dough in a bowl, cover with damp cloth and set aside for 30 minutes.

Heat the oil in a small saucepan over high heat until the oil reaches about 180°C/456°F. (To check whether the oil is hot enough, hold a wooden chopstick in the oil. If it is immediately surrounded by tiny bubbles, the oil is ready to use.) Place the spring onions (scallions) in a small bowl and pour the hot oil over the top to make scallion oil.

Divide the dough into 4 portions and shape each into a round. Using a rolling pin, roll out one round on a lightly floured surface until very thin. Brush with scallion oil and sprinkle with a pinch of salt and five-spice.

Carefully roll up the thin dough round, pull the roll a little longer with your hands, then encircle the roll around one end to form a dough spiral that resembles a cinnamon roll. Flatten the spiral with your palm to make a round pancake. Repeat with the remaining dough portions.

Heat a non-stick frying pan over medium heat until hot. Add a pancake, reduce heat to low and cook for 2–3 minutes or until one side is golden. Flip and repeat to cook the other side. Repeat with remaining pancakes.

Danish butter bread:

PREPARATION TIME
30 minutes

COOKING TIME
5 minutes

SERVES
2

If you watch a film set in twentieth-century Shanghai, you might see street scenes at night featuring vendors with large steaming pots, cooking freshly made wonton soup. This comforting dish is traditionally enjoyed as a late-night snack or breakfast.

This style of wonton, called 'small wontons', is traditionally made with minced pork. ('Big wontons', made with local meat and vegetables, are prepared a bit differently.) They are cooked very quickly and served in a hot soup, then topped with egg slices, dried shrimp, seaweed and spring onion. In this vegan version, I use vegan mince and vegetable stock.

上海小馄饨

SHANGHAI XIAO HUNTUN (SHANGHAI WONTON SOUP)

- 10 g (¼ oz) fresh ginger, finely chopped
- 200 g (7 oz) vegan mince
- 2 tablespoons soy sauce
- 1 tablespoon vegan oyster sauce
- 1 teaspoon ground white pepper
- 30 wonton wrappers
- ½ teaspoon salt
- 1 tablespoon sesame oil
- ½ teaspoon Chinese five-spice
- 800 ml (27 fl oz) vegetable stock
- 10 g (¼ oz) nori (dried seaweed), crushed
- 2 spring onions (scallions), sliced, to serve

Mix the ginger with 90 ml (3 fl oz) of water and set aside for 5 minutes, then strain, reserving the ginger water. Mix the vegan mince, reserved ginger water, soy sauce, vegan oyster sauce and ½ teaspoon of the ground white pepper in a bowl.

Take a wonton wrapper on your palm, place a teaspoon of the vegan mince mixture on the wrapper, then press your thumb and index finger together to close the wrapper. If the wrapper is too dry and does not close, sprinkle a little water on the edge and seal to close. Set aside on a lined tray while you repeat with remaining wrappers to make 30 wontons.

Divide the salt, sesame oil, five-spice and remaining pepper between two serving bowls.

Bring the vegetable stock to the boil in a pot over medium heat. Add the nori and wontons, and cook for 1–2 minutes until they float. Divide the wontons and the soup between the bowls. Sprinkle with spring onions to serve.

PREPARATION TIME
2–3 hours

COOKING TIME
15 minutes

MAKES
30

Originally from Shanghai, shengjian bao has gained fame around the world. It is similar to bao'zi (steamed bao buns), but smaller, and the dough is not left to rise for as long, so the wrapping is thinner and less fluffy.

Like the small wontons, traditional shengjian bao has only one filling: minced pork. Vegan mince makes a delicious alternative.

生煎包

SHENGJIAN BAO (PAN-FRIED BAO)

- 300 g (10½ oz) plain (all-purpose) wheat flour
- 1 teaspoon instant dried yeast
- ½ teaspoon baking powder
- 50 ml (1¾ fl oz) plant-based milk
- 10 g (¼ oz) fresh ginger, finely chopped
- 2 spring onions (scallions), sliced
- 300 g (10½ oz) vegan mince
- 2 tablespoons cooking wine
- 1 tablespoon sesame oil
- 3 tablespoons soy sauce
- 1 tablespoon vegan oyster sauce
- ½ teaspoon salt
- 1 teaspoon Chinese five-spice
- ½ teaspoon ground white pepper
- 2 tablespoons canola (rapeseed) oil
- 1 tablespoon toasted sesame seeds

To make the dough, mix the flour, yeast, baking powder, milk and 100 ml (3½ fl oz) of water in a large bowl and knead to form a smooth dough. Cover with a damp tea towel (dish towel) and set aside to rise until the dough is doubled in size. Depending on the temperature in your kitchen, this could take anywhere from about 45 minutes up to 2 hours. Knead the dough again for 1–2 minutes to punch out any bubbles and divide into 30 portions.

Meanwhile, mix the ginger, half the spring onion and 120 ml (4 fl oz) of water in a small bowl. Set aside to soak for 5 minutes, then strain and discard the ginger and spring onion, reserving the water. Mix the vegan mince with the reserved ginger water, cooking wine, sesame oil, soy sauce, vegan oyster sauce, salt, five-spice and pepper.

Using a rolling pin, roll each of the 30 dough portions into a flat, round wrap (the edge should be slightly thinner than the centre). Take a tablespoon of the vegan mince mixture and place it in the middle of the wrap, then close the wrap completely by simply gathering the edges together or by creating pleats. Set aside on a tray and repeat to make 30 buns. Cover with a damp tea towel and set aside to rest for 15 minutes.

Add one-third of the canola oil and 10 buns to a non-stick frying pan. Place pan over low–medium heat. Pan-fry until the bases of the buns are golden (lift one up to check), then pour in enough water to reach one-quarter of the height of the buns. Cover the pan and cook for a few more minutes until the water has evaporated. Sprinkle the buns with sesame seeds and remaining spring onion and pan-fry for another 1–2 minutes, uncovered, until the bases are crispy again. Remove from heat and repeat with remaining two batches of 10.

PREPARATION TIME
1 hour

COOKING TIME
30 minutes

MAKES
8

Jiucai hezi are quite famous in the north of China. The dough is cut, rolled into wraps and usually filled with garlic chives (Chinese chives) and scrambled eggs. For the vegan version, I use scrambled tofu instead of egg and kala namak (Himalayan black salt) to add an eggy flavour.

These are commonly sold at small shops and street stands, alongside other savoury pastries. They're typically enjoyed as a quick breakfast or snack on the go. They're the perfect combination: affordable, filling and satisfying.

Garlic chives are widely used in China, where they are treated more like a vegetable than a herb.

韭菜盒子

JIUCAI HEZI (GARLIC CHIVE POCKETS)

- 20 g (¾ oz) dried glass noodles
- 300 g (10½ oz) plain (all-purpose) wheat flour, plus extra for dusting
- ½ teaspoon salt
- 75 ml (2½ fl oz) canola (rapeseed) oil
- 150 g (5½ oz) semi-firm tofu
- ½ teaspoon kala namak (Himalayan black salt)
- 50 g (1¾ oz) garlic chives (Chinese chives), chopped
- 1 tablespoon sesame oil
- ½ teaspoon Chinese five-spice

Soak the noodles in water for 10 minutes, then drain and chop.

Mix flour, salt and 150 ml (5 fl oz) of water in a large bowl and knead to form a dough. Cover with a damp tea towel (dish towel) and set aside to rest for 30 minutes.

Heat a wok over medium heat and, once hot, add 2 tablespoons of the canola oil. Add the tofu, breaking it up with a spatula, and stir-fry for 1 minute. Add kala namak, mix everything and stir-fry for 1–2 minutes.

Add garlic chives and noodles to a large bowl, then add the scrambled tofu, sesame oil and five-spice and mix well.

Roll out the dough on a lightly floured surface into a long, thick, cylindrical length and cut it into 8 even portions.

Press a portion of dough flat with your palm and use a rolling pin to make it round and thin. Add about 2 tablespoons of the filling to the centre of the wrap (don't overfill or it will be hard to close), then fold and seal carefully, like a dumpling. Repeat with remaining dough portions.

Heat a non-stick frying pan over medium heat until hot, then add half the remaining canola oil. Pan-fry four garlic chive pockets for 1–2 minutes. Add 100 ml (3½ fl oz) of hot water, cover and cook for a further 2–3 minutes. Uncover and cook until all the water has evaporated. Turn the chive pockets over and continue pan-frying them for about 2–3 minutes until they are golden and slightly crispy on both sides. Repeat with the remaining canola oil and pockets.

PREPARATION TIME
15 minutes

COOKING TIME
40 minutes

SERVES
2 (makes 6 noodle sheets diameter 24 cm/9½ in)

These rice-noodle rolls, which are naturally vegan, are a Cantonese dim sum and street food. There are many ways to cook them, including stir-frying or using a clay pot. They are commonly mixed with three different sauces, the combination of which brings out multiple layers of rich flavour.

During my school years in Guangzhou, there were always street trolleys selling these rice-noodle rolls around the corner from my school. They were so cheap and satisfying!

三酱猪肠粉

JYU CHEUNG FUN (THREE-SAUCE RICE-NOODLE ROLLS)

- 200 g (7 oz) rice flour
- 2½ tablespoons cornflour (cornstarch)
- 30 g (1 oz) wheat starch
- 1 tablespoon canola (rapeseed) oil
- 1 tablespoon toasted white sesame seeds

FIRST SAUCE

- 1½ tablespoons sesame paste
- 1 tablespoon peanut butter
- 2 tablespoons sesame oil

SECOND SAUCE

- 2 tablespoons light soy sauce
- ½ tablespoon dark soy sauce
- 1 tablespoon vegan oyster sauce
- 1 teaspoon sugar
- 1 tablespoon canola (rapeseed) oil
- 20 g (¾ oz) onion, sliced

THIRD SAUCE

- 3 tablespoons hoisin sauce
- 1 tablespoon tomato sauce (ketchup)
- 1 teaspoon sugar

Mix the rice flour, cornflour, wheat starch and 500 ml (17 fl oz/ 2 cups) of water in a large bowl. Pass the batter through a sieve to remove any small lumps, as these will cause your noodles to be lumpy after steaming.

Brush a little of the canola oil over a flat, heatproof plate (stainless steel is ideal) that will fit inside a saucepan. Fill the saucepan with hot water and place a steam rack inside (the water level should not be higher than the steam rack).

Place the prepared plate on top of the steam rack, cover and let it steam over high heat for 30 seconds, then take the plate out (using a plate holder), mix the batter again and pour a thin layer onto the plate. The plate should be hot when the batter is poured on, so that the rice noodle sheet does not crack while steaming.

Place the plate back on the steam rack, cover and let it steam for 3–5 minutes. (The exact time will depend on the thickness of both your batter and the plate.)

When the noodle sheet has become completely translucent and you can see big bubbles forming under the noodle sheet, carefully take out the plate. Fill a large bowl or container with cold water and float the plate in the water for a couple of minutes to cool it down.

⟶

Once it cools down, remove the noodle sheet carefully (if it is still hot, it will be sticky and difficult to peel off the plate). Roll the noodle sheet up, with the bottom side facing out. Cut the noodle roll into 4 cm (1½ in) lengths and set aside.

Repeat until all the batter has been steamed.

While the noodle sheets are being steamed, prepare the sauces. To make the first sauce, mix the sesame paste, peanut butter and sesame oil in a small bowl to form a smooth paste. Add 3 tablespoons of hot water and continue mixing until smooth.

To make the second sauce, mix the light soy sauce, dark soy sauce, vegan oyster sauce, sugar and 3 tablespoons of water in another bowl. Heat a saucepan over medium heat and, once hot, add the canola oil and onion. Cook, stirring, for 30 seconds, then add the soy sauce mixture and cook for 2 minutes. Remove from heat.

To make the third sauce, mix the hoisin sauce, tomato sauce, sugar and 2 tablespoons of water in a saucepan over medium heat. Bring to the boil then remove from heat immediately.

Transfer rice-noodle rolls to serving bowls and pour over all three sauces. Sprinkle with sesame seeds to serve.

石板街
台湾绝
秋刀鱼

PREPARATION TIME
12 hours

COOKING TIME
10 minutes

SERVES
2

The name of this beloved dish comes from the pungent smell and flavour of tofu after fermentation. There are different kinds of stinky tofu. Most are light in colour and deep-fried, but others are softer, resembling the texture of preserved and fermented bean curd.

This version is a simple recipe that doesn't require you to make the marinade yourself. The crucial ingredient is the sauce made by the brand Wangzhihe. A fermented bean curd, this condiment is a staple in Chinese cuisine and widely available at Chinese grocers.

臭豆腐
CHOU DOUFU (STINKY TOFU)

- 100 g (3½ oz) Wangzhihe preserved bean curd in cooking sauce (王致和臭豆腐乳), liquid from jar reserved
- 600 g (1 lb 5 oz) bean curd/firm tofu, sliced about 5 mm (¼ in) thick or diced about 2 cm (¾ in) thick
- 360 ml (12 fl oz) canola (rapeseed) oil
- 5 garlic cloves, finely chopped
- 4 birdseye chillies, destemmed and finely chopped
- 2 tablespoons chilli flakes
- 90 ml (3 fl oz) vegetable stock
- 2 tablespoons soy sauce
- 1 teaspoon Chinese five-spice
- 1 teaspoon sugar
- 2 tablespoons Chilli oil (page 23)
- 30 g (1 oz) pickled radish, chopped
- 1 spring onion (scallion), sliced
- 1 coriander (cilantro) sprig, chopped

Place the preserved bean curd in an airtight container and break up with a spoon. Add 200 ml (7 fl oz) of water, 100 ml (3½ fl oz) of the reserved liquid from the jar and the tofu slices, ensuring the tofu is covered. Put on the lid and refrigerate overnight.

Put the tofu slices on a wire rack set over a baking tray and leave to dry for 15 minutes (if the tofu is too wet, it will cause oil splashes while frying).

Meanwhile, to make the sauce, heat a saucepan over medium–high heat and, once hot, add 60 ml (2 fl oz/¼ cup) of the canola oil, the garlic and birdseye chilli. Cook, stirring, until aromatic, then add chilli flakes and cook, stirring, for 30 seconds. Add the vegetable stock, soy sauce, five-spice and sugar. Cook for 2–3 minutes, then remove from heat.

Heat the remaining canola oil in a large saucepan over medium–high heat. To check whether the oil is hot enough for deep-frying, hold a wooden chopstick in the oil. If it is immediately surrounded by tiny bubbles, the oil is ready to use. Keep the oil temperature steady for deep-frying.

Add the tofu slices, one at a time, and fry until crisp. Remove using a slotted spoon or a sieve, drain the oil and place on a serving plate. Pour over the sauce and top with chilli oil, pickled radish, spring onion and coriander to serve.

PREPARATION TIME
5 minutes

COOKING TIME
10 minutes

SERVES
2

Sizzling tofu is a street food you'll likely find at every night market in China. Tofu is seared on a hot iron plate ('tieban'), giving it slight crispiness on the outside and hot, smooth juiciness on the inside.

When you buy this dish from a street vendor, the sizzling sound and rising steam add to the experience. As the tofu cooks, it's drizzled with seasonings, creating a mouthwatering combination of spicy, salty and umami flavours. It's one of the most tempting vegan street foods you'll find, especially on a cold day.

铁板豆腐

TIEBAN DOUFU (SIZZLING TOFU)

- 90 ml (3 fl oz) canola (rapeseed) oil
- 600 g (1 lb 5 oz) tender or semi-firm tofu, sliced about ½ cm (¼ in) thick
- 2 tablespoons ground cumin
- 2 tablespoons ground chilli
- 2 teaspoons Chinese five-spice
- 1 teaspoon salt
- 2 spring onions (scallions), sliced
- coriander (cilantro) leaves, to garnish

Heat a flat, non-stick frying pan over high heat. Once hot, add the oil and tofu and fry for 2–3 minutes until one side is slightly brown and crispy. Carefully turn over.

Reduce heat to medium, sprinkle the tofu evenly with the cumin, chilli, five-spice and salt. Cook for another 1–2 minutes, then sprinkle with spring onion and coriander to serve.

PREPARATION TIME
1 hour

COOKING TIME
30 minutes

SERVES
4

Barbecue is highly renowned in China, especially at the night markets. No matter which city you're in, there are always skewered meats and vegetables being prepared on a charcoal grill, and people sitting around small tables on the roadside, drinking beer while enjoying the street barbecue.

The ingredients and seasonings used in barbecue differ greatly between regions; however, cumin and chilli flakes are widely used. Here, I am sharing a recipe for Hunan-style barbecue. You'll find fresh tofu skin (baiye tofu) sheets in Asian stores.

街头烧烤 JIETOU SHAOKAO (STREET BARBECUE)

- 5 small potatoes, peeled
- 6 king oyster mushrooms
- 1 head garlic (10–12 cloves), finely chopped
- 100 ml (3½ fl oz) canola (rapeseed) oil
- 150 ml (5 fl oz) soy sauce
- 50 ml (1¾ fl oz) vegan oyster sauce
- 100 g (3½ oz) fresh tofu skin (baiye tofu) sheets
- 2 corn cobs
- 200 g (7 oz) garlic chives
- 50 g (1¾ oz) cumin seeds
- 100 g (3½ oz) chilli flakes or ground chilli
- 5 spring onions (scallions), sliced

Cut the potatoes and king oyster mushrooms into thin slices (the potato slices need to be about 2 mm/⅛ in thick, and the mushrooms about 5 mm/¼ in thick). Mix the garlic and oil in a small bowl and set aside. Mix the soy sauce and vegan oyster sauce in another small bowl.

Cut the tofu skin into smaller sheets, about 10 cm (4 in) x 8 cm (3 in).

Bring a saucepan of water to the boil and cook the potato slices for 2 minutes, then drain and place in cold water to soak. Add 90 ml (3 fl oz) of the sauce mixture to the mushroom slices, mix and let them marinate for 15 minutes.

Preheat grill to hot. Thread the potato, mushroom and tofu skin onto skewers and brush all over with the garlic oil. Add skewers, corn and garlic chives to the grill, turning to cook evenly. The cooking time depends on how strong the heat is. Generally, the potato and corn take the longest (5–8 minutes) while the garlic chives and tofu skin only take about 2 minutes.

When the vegetables are halfway through cooking, brush all over with remaining sauce mixture and continue to grill until almost fully cooked.

Sprinkle cumin seeds and chilli flakes over the vegetables, turning to coat evenly. Grill for another 30 seconds until fully cooked, then sprinkle with spring onion and serve.

PREPARATION TIME
30 minutes

COOKING TIME
20 minutes

SERVES
2

Malatang is loved all over China for its bold, spicy flavours. 'Ma' means mouth-numbing (from the sichuan peppercorns), 'la' means spicy (from the chilli) and 'tang' means hot, because the broth is always boiling. 'Mala' is regarded as the most representative flavour profile of Sichuan food.

At a malatang stand, you can choose from dozens of different ingredients (vegetables, meats, tofu and noodles) to be cooked quickly in the hot, red broth. I've simplified this recipe by using a store-bought hotpot paste. From the Asian store, you will also need doubanjiang (for more on this ingredient, see page 60).

麻辣烫

MALATANG (SPICY HOTPOT)

- 2 tablespoons canola (rapeseed) oil
- 3 garlic cloves, chopped
- 2 tablespoons whole sichuan peppercorns
- 100 g (3½ oz) doubanjiang (fermented broad bean and chilli paste)
- 300 g (10½ oz) spicy sichuan hotpot paste (vegan)
- 1.5 litres (51 fl oz/6 cups) vegetable stock
- 1 tablespoon sugar
- 200 g (7 oz) potatoes
- 200 g (7 oz) lotus root
- 10 fresh shiitake mushrooms
- 200 g (7 oz) enoki mushrooms
- 200 g (7 oz) oyster mushrooms
- 200 g (7 oz) semi-firm or firm tofu
- 2 heads pak choi
- 200 g (7 oz) water spinach
- 10 tofu puffs
- 120 g (4½ oz) rice noodles or glass noodles, soaked in water and drained, or instant noodles
- 2 coriander (cilantro) sprigs, chopped
- 3 spring onions (scallions), chopped
- 80 g (2¾ oz) sesame paste
- 2 tablespoons Chilli oil (page 23)

Heat a wok over medium heat and, once hot, add the oil. Add the garlic and sichuan peppercorns, then stir for 1 minute until aromatic. Add the doubanjiang and stir for 1 minute, then add the hotpot paste and stir for another minute.

Add the vegetable stock and sugar and bring to the boil. Reduce heat to low and simmer for 5 minutes.

Meanwhile, peel and slice the potatoes and lotus root. Score the caps of the shiitake mushrooms, and roughly slice the enoki and oyster mushrooms. Slice the semi-firm or firm tofu. Separate the pak choi leaves and cut the water spinach into 8 cm (3¼ in) lengths.

To the simmering broth, add the potato, lotus root, sliced tofu, tofu puffs and mushrooms, and continue simmering for a few minutes. Add the noodles and cook according to packet instructions. When the noodles are almost cooked, add the pak choi leaves and water spinach, cook for 30 seconds.

Divide the broth and ingredients between two serving bowls. Top with the coriander sprigs, spring onion, sesame paste and chilli oil to serve.

PREPARATION TIME
10 minutes

COOKING TIME
20 minutes

SERVES
2

Guoba potato is another widely loved street food from Sichuan. 'Guoba' normally means 'rice crust', but it can also refer to other crusty or crispy foods. In this dish, the potatoes are first boiled, then deep-fried, resulting in chunks that are crisp and golden on the outside, but soft and tender inside. Once you mix the potatoes with the sauce, the dish has many layers of flavour and texture.

锅巴土豆
GUOBA TUDOU (GUOBA POTATO)

- 800 g (1 lb 12 oz) potatoes, peeled and cut into chunks about 3 cm (1¼ in) wide
- 3 tablespoons potato starch or cornflour (cornstarch)
- 2 tablespoons plain (all-purpose) wheat flour
- 3 garlic cloves, finely chopped
- 1 tablespoon ground cumin
- 1 teaspoon ground sichuan peppercorns
- ½ teaspoon salt
- 1 tablespoon chilli flakes or ground chilli
- 1 tablespoon toasted white sesame seeds
- 600 ml (20½ fl oz) canola (rapeseed) oil
- 3 tablespoons soy sauce
- 2 tablespoons Chilli oil (page 23)
- 2 spring onions (scallions), sliced
- coriander (cilantro) leaves, to garnish

Bring a large saucepan of water to the boil. Add potato and cook for 10 minutes. Drain, then return the potato to the pan, add the potato starch or cornflour and wheat flour and mix well to combine.

Mix the garlic, cumin, sichuan peppercorns, salt, chilli flakes and sesame seeds in a large bowl.

Heat the canola oil in a large saucepan over medium–high heat. To check whether the oil is hot enough for deep-frying, hold a wooden chopstick in the oil. If it is immediately surrounded by tiny bubbles, the oil is ready to use. Keep the oil temperature steady for deep-frying.

Carefully spoon about 2 tablespoons of the hot oil over the garlic and spice mixture. Add soy sauce. Add potato to the remaining hot oil and fry for about 15 minutes until golden and crispy. Remove the potato with a slotted spoon or a sieve and transfer to the bowl with the spices. Add chilli oil, spring onion and coriander and mix everything well.

PREPARATION TIME
1 hour

COOKING TIME
15 minutes

MAKES
4

This dish, which translates to 'pancake with fragrant sauce', is often enjoyed as a quick breakfast or a light lunch. The rich sauce is brushed on the flat dough, which is heated on a griddle. Once cooked, the outer layer of the dough becomes slightly crisp while the inside is tender.

Traditionally vegan, jiang xiang bing is defined by its rich, tangy sauce, which brings all the other ingredients together in a delicious package. Doubanjiang, a spicy, salty condiment made from fermented broad beans, is an essential condiment in Sichuan cuisine. The most famous variety is from Pixian, a district of Chengdu.

酱香饼
JIANG XIANG BING (SAVOURY PANCAKE)

- 110 ml (4 fl oz) canola (rapeseed) oil, plus extra for brushing
- 4 garlic cloves, finely chopped
- 10 g (¼ oz) fresh ginger, finely chopped
- 50 g (1¾ oz) onion, finely chopped
- 300 g (10½ oz) plain (all-purpose) wheat flour, plus 50 g (1¾ oz) extra
- ½ teaspoon salt
- ½ teaspoon thirteen-spice
- 2 spring onions (scallions), sliced
- 1 tablespoon toasted white sesame seeds

SAUCE

- 2 tablespoons doubanjiang (fermented broad bean and chilli paste)
- 1 tablespoon soybean paste
- 1 tablespoon tomato sauce (ketchup)
- 2 tablespoons vegan oyster sauce
- 1 teaspoon sugar
- 1 tablespoon chilli flakes
- ½ teaspoon Chinese five-spice

To make the sauce, mix the doubanjiang, soybean paste, tomato sauce, vegan oyster sauce, sugar, chilli flakes, five-spice and 90 ml (3 fl oz) of water in a bowl and set aside.

Heat a non-stick frying pan over medium heat. Once hot, add 30 ml (1 fl oz/2 tablespoons) of the oil, plus the garlic, ginger and onion, and stir until aromatic. Add the sauce and cook for 1 minute.

Using a chopstick, mix the flour, salt and 80 ml (2½ fl oz/⅓ cup) of hot water in a bowl, then add 80 ml (2½ fl oz/⅓ cup) of room-temperature water and knead to form a dough. Brush with a little extra oil, then place in a clean bowl, cover and set aside to rest for 30 minutes.

In a separate heatproof bowl, mix the extra 50 g (1¾ oz) of flour with the thirteen-spice. Heat 50 ml (1¾ fl oz) of the oil in a small saucepan over high heat until very hot (about 170°C/338°F). Pour it over the flour-spice mixture and mix well to combine.

Brush the kitchen surface and your hands with a little extra oil to prevent sticking, then separate the dough into 4 portions and shape each into a round (put more oil on your hands if the dough starts to stick). Add 2 tablespoons of the oiled flour to each round. Using a rolling pin, roll out each round into a thin sheet to form a pancake.

Heat a non-stick frying pan over medium heat and, once hot, add 30 ml (1 fl oz/2 tablespoons) of oil. Add a pancake and cook for 2–3 minutes or until the bottom is golden and crisp, then flip. Brush a thin layer of sauce on the pancake and cook until the other side is also golden and crisp. Repeat with remaining pancakes. Sprinkle with spring onion and sesame seeds to serve.

PREPARATION TIME
20 minutes

COOKING TIME
5 minutes

SERVES
2

Fried chicken fingers are a classic street food at the night market. For this vegan version, I use oyster mushrooms, which make for a juicy and satisfying alternative to meat. Super crisp on the outside and tender on the inside, they are a wonderful snack to share with family or friends.

素炸鸡柳

SU ZHA JI LIU (FRIED VEGAN 'CHICKEN' FINGERS)

- 500 g (1 lb 2 oz) oyster mushrooms
- 2 teaspoons salt
- 2 teaspoons Chinese five-spice
- ½ teaspoon ground black pepper
- 2 teaspoons garlic powder
- 100 ml (3½ fl oz) sparkling water
- 100 g (3½ oz) cornflour (cornstarch)
- 500 ml (17 fl oz/2 cups) canola (rapeseed) oil
- 2 teaspoons ground chilli
- 2 teaspoons ground cumin

Using your hands, break the oyster mushrooms into strips about 1 cm (½ in) wide and add to a bowl. Add salt, five-spice, black pepper and garlic powder, mix everything well and set aside to marinate for 15 minutes.

Add the sparkling water to the mushrooms and mix well. Add cornflour and toss to coat the mushrooms.

Heat the oil in a large saucepan over medium–high heat. To check whether the oil is hot enough for deep-frying, hold a wooden chopstick in the oil. If it is immediately surrounded by tiny bubbles, the oil is ready to use. Keep the oil temperature steady for deep-frying.

Add mushrooms to the pan and deep-fry for 3–5 minutes until golden on the outside, then remove using a slotted spoon or a sieve and place on a serving dish. Sprinkle with chilli and cumin to serve.

PREPARATION TIME
15 minutes

COOKING TIME
10 minutes

SERVES
2

There are many different varieties of ciba, a sweet treat made with glutinous rice that is well-known in the southern regions of China. Hongtang ciba is from Sichuan and is often served alongside hotpot, with bingfen (page 73).

Just like mochi (page 210), ciba is traditionally made by pounding the rice into a paste in a large stone mortar. Today, this laborious method is only used in the villages, or around Chinese New Year when families are making a lot of ciba to give to relatives and friends. This pan-fried version requires very few ingredients and is quick to make.

红糖糍粑

HONGTANG CIBA (BROWN SUGAR CIBA CAKE)

- 200 g (7 oz) glutinous rice flour
- 1 tablespoon sugar
- 60 g (2 oz) soft brown sugar
- 2 tablespoons canola (rapeseed) oil
- 2 tablespoons kinako (toasted soybean flour)

Mix the glutinous rice flour and the 1 tablespoon of sugar in a large bowl. Gradually add 160 ml (5½ fl oz) of lukewarm water, while stirring with a chopstick. Knead into a smooth dough, then transfer the dough to a flat surface and, using a rolling pin, roll out to about 1.5 cm (½ in) thick. Cut the flat dough into strips about 1.5 cm (½ in) wide and 5 cm (2 in) long.

To make the brown sugar syrup, mix the soft brown sugar and 50 ml (1¾ fl oz) of water in a small saucepan over low heat. Cook for 3 minutes, stirring, until the sugar is dissolved. Remove from heat.

Heat a non-stick frying pan over low–medium heat and, once hot, add the oil. Add the ciba strips, allowing space between them to prevent sticking, and pan-fry, turning, until both sides are golden and crispy. Transfer to a serving plate, sprinkle with kinako and pour over the brown sugar syrup.

PREPARATION TIME
5 minutes

COOKING TIME
10 minutes

MAKES
6

'Tanghulu' literally means 'sugar calabash' because the snack resembles the shape of a bottle gourd. Traditionally, tanghulu was made with Chinese hawberries, sour little red fruits that provide the ideal contrast to the sweetness of the sugar.

Today, tanghulu stands have shelves of these skewers made with all kinds of fruits: strawberries, tangerines, mulberries, blueberries, kiwis, plums ... the options are limitless. Try these with any fruit you like, or even a combination of different fruits. They're very pretty.

- 6 Chinese hawberries
- 6 strawberries
- 6 green grapes
- 400 g (14 oz) sugar

糖葫芦

TANGHULU (CANDIED HAWTHORN SKEWERS)

Push 3 fruits carefully onto each of 6 bamboo skewers. Place on a tray lined with baking paper and put in the freezer for 10 minutes.

Meanwhile, mix the sugar and 100 ml (3½ fl oz) of water in a non-stick frying pan over low–medium heat and cook until the sugar is dissolved and the temperature reaches about 160°/320°F). Do not stir too much during this process. Once the sugar is slightly browned, immediately turn off the heat.

Remove the skewers from the freezer. Dip the skewered fruits in the syrup, turning them to ensure they are evenly coated (work quickly here, otherwise the syrup might crystallise or harden). If the syrup starts to harden before all the fruits are dipped, heat it up over low heat until it's liquid again, but be very careful not to overheat it or it will turn dark and bitter.

Put the tanghulu back on the tray lined with baking paper or on another non-stick surface for 2 minutes to allow the syrup to set.

PREPARATION TIME
15 minutes

COOKING TIME
15 minutes

MAKES
2 glasses, each 500 ml
(17 fl oz/2 cups)

Zhenzhu naicha needs no introduction. It's been the most famous drink in China for years, especially among young people. You can probably see a bubble tea shop on every street in the centre of a Chinese city and there are always stands at the night markets. Today, you can buy the drink with all kinds of tea, fillings and toppings. Here, I am sharing a recipe for the original bubble tea, using black tea mixed with milk and brown sugar. Sago (tapioca) pearls are available from most Asian stores, or you can make your own using tapioca flour.

珍珠奶茶

ZHENZHU NAICHA (BUBBLE TEA)

- 50 g (1¾ oz) white sugar
- 20 g (¾ oz) black ceylon tea
- 1 tablespoon soft brown sugar
- 60 g (2 oz) sago (tapioca) pearls
- 200 ml (7 fl oz) plant-based milk
- 300 g (10½ oz) ice cubes

Mix 60 ml (2 fl oz/¼ cup) of water and the white sugar in a saucepan over low heat until the sugar is dissolved. Cook for 2–3 minutes, without stirring, or until the mixture thickens. Set aside to cool.

Mix 500 ml (17 fl oz/2 cups) of water and the tea leaves in a saucepan over low heat. Bring to the boil and cook for 10 minutes. Strain the tea leaves with a strainer or a sieve. Set aside to cool.

Mix the soft brown sugar with 100 ml (3½ fl oz) of hot water. Cook the sago pearls according to packet instructions, then drain and add the pearls to the brown sugar water.

Divide the sago pearls, syrup, tea, milk and ice between two glasses.

PREPARATION TIME
15 minutes

COOKING TIME
5 minutes

MAKES
2 glasses, each 500 ml (17 fl oz/2 cups)

One of the most popular summer drinks in China is the boldly named 暴打柠檬茶, which translates to 'violently smacked lemon tea'. You'll find stands selling it in nearly every night market across the country.

Traditionally, it's made with Ya Shi Xiang, a partially fermented oolong tea from Chaozhou in Canton. Despite its unusual name – which literally means 'duck shit fragrance' – this tea is prized for its floral and subtly fruity aroma. The lemons typically used are known as 'perfume lemons', recognisable by their thick peel, green colour, intense fragrance and milder acidity compared to regular lemons. In this version of the recipe, I have used jasmine green tea, lime and lemon because they are easier to find.

暴打柠檬茶
BAODA NINGMENG CHA (HAND-SMACKED LEMON TEA)

- 60 g (2 oz) sugar
- 20 g (¾ oz) jasmine green tea
- 1 lemon, sliced and deseeded
- 1 lime, sliced
- 300 g (10½ oz) ice cubes

Mix sugar with 60 ml (2 fl oz/¼ cup) of water in a small saucepan over low heat until the sugar is dissolved. Cook for 2–3 minutes, without stirring, until the mixture thickens. Remove from heat and set aside to cool.

Add the tea to a pot or a heatproof bowl and add 500 ml (17 fl oz/ 2 cups) of hot water (85–90°C/185–190°F). Cover and leave to steep for 10 minutes, then strain the tea leaves with a strainer or a sieve. Set aside to cool.

Mix the lemon and lime in a cocktail shaker and smack them with a muddler. Add the sugar syrup and half the ice cubes, and keep smacking the fruits with the ice cubes for 15 seconds. Add the tea and shake vigorously for 30 seconds.

Divide the remaining ice cubes and the tea from the shaker between two glasses.

PREPARATION TIME
15 minutes, plus 4 hours chilling

COOKING TIME
5 minutes

SERVES
2

One of the most popular street desserts in China, the original bingfen from Sichuan is very simple: brown sugar syrup is poured over jelly and topped with raisins, haw flakes and a sprinkle of peanuts.

Traditionally, the jelly is made with the seeds of *Nicandra physalodes* (sometimes called the shoo-fly plant). Although this recipe tastes great, the method is time-consuming, so many vendors use packaged ice jelly powder, which you can buy from Asian stores. I've used the same powder : water ratio as the one suggested by a well-known brand, but check the packet instructions of the brand you're using. Top your bingfen with anything you like, such as red or mung beans, sago or taro balls.

冰粉

BINGFEN (ICE JELLY)

- 15 g (½ oz) ice jelly powder
- 80 g (2¾ oz) soft brown sugar
- 1 tablespoon raisins
- 1 tablespoon unsalted peanuts, crushed
- 30 g (1 oz) haw flakes, diced
- 200 g (7 oz) watermelon, diced
- 200 g (7 oz) mango, diced

Mix ice jelly powder with 1 litre (34 fl oz/4 cups) of hot water in a large saucepan over high heat and mix until dissolved. Bring to the boil, then remove from heat and set aside to cool. Once cooled, refrigerate for at least 4 hours.

Bring 100 ml (3½ fl oz) of water to the boil in another saucepan over high heat. Add soft brown sugar and mix until dissolved. Reduce heat to low and cook for 2 minutes.

Divide the ice jelly, brown sugar syrup, raisins, peanuts, haw flakes, watermelon and mango between two serving bowls.

THAILAND

From grilled skewers and pad thai (page 76) to som tam (green papaya salad, page 90) and khao niew mamuang (mango sticky rice, page 104), the variety of authentic street food in Thailand makes it a culinary heaven for locals and tourists. The street food scene serves as a window into the nation's diversity and rich traditions, with each region contributing unique specialities. Fresh herbs and spices are used widely.

In cities like Bangkok, Chiang Mai and Phuket, you can find street food around just about every corner. Some of Bangkok's hotspots include Chinatown, Jodd Fairs, Srinakarin Train Market, Samyan Market next to the renowned Chulalongkorn University, and Asiatique Riverfront on the Chao Phraya riverside.

In Chiang Mai, the most visited street food markets are the Chiang Mai Night Bazaar, the Nimmanhaemin Road Night Market and the Tha Pae Walking Street, held every Sunday. The places to go in Phuket are the Phuket Old Town Night Market, Malin Plaza Patong and Karon Temple Market.

Many street food dishes can be made vegan – just ask for the meat to be swapped with tofu and the fish sauce to be omitted.

PREPARATION TIME
15 minutes

COOKING TIME
10 minutes

SERVES
2

One of the most famous Thai dishes, and a classic street food in Thailand, pad thai is loved for its mix of bold flavours and simple ingredients.

Served hot off the wok, with lime, bean sprouts, chilli flakes and crunchy peanuts, this is the kind of dish you can grab from a street vendor and enjoy right away. It's easy, satisfying and packed with the flavours that make Thai food so loved.

This version, which uses vegan fish sauce, is just as tasty as the original.

ผัดไทย

PAD THAI (STIR-FRIED RICE NOODLES)

- 400 g (14 oz) fresh thin rice noodles or 200 g (7 oz) dried rice noodles (width 3 mm/⅛ in)
- 1 tablespoon coconut (palm) sugar
- 75 ml (2½ fl oz) tamarind sauce
- 40 ml (1¼ fl oz) Vegan fish sauce (page 18)
- 60 ml (2 fl oz/¼ cup) canola (rapeseed) oil
- 3 garlic cloves, chopped
- 2 shallots, sliced
- 30 g (1 oz) preserved radish, chopped
- 300 g (10½ oz) pan-fried tofu, sliced
- 150 g (5½ oz) bean sprouts
- 100 g (3½ oz) garlic chives, cut into 3 cm (1¼ in) lengths
- 100 g (3½ oz) roasted and salted peanuts, crushed
- 1 tablespoon chilli flakes
- 1 lime, halved
- banana leaves, for serving (optional)

If you're using dried noodles, soak in lukewarm water for 30 minutes, then drain. Skip this step if you're using fresh noodles.

In a bowl, mix the coconut sugar, tamarind sauce and vegan fish sauce.

Heat a wok over high heat and, once hot, add the oil, garlic, shallot and preserved radish. Stir for 1 minute until aromatic.

Add the noodles, and stir for 30 seconds to 1 minute until they start to soften. Add the tamarind sauce mixture and the tofu, and mix with chopsticks. Continue to mix for 1–2 minutes until the noodles have mostly softened.

Add three-quarters of the bean sprouts and stir for 30 seconds. Then, add three-quarters of the garlic chives and stir for 30 seconds more.

Transfer to serving bowls and top with crushed peanuts, chilli and the remaining garlic chives and bean sprouts. (Alternatively, arrange on banana leaves.) Squeeze some lime juice over the noodles and mix everything together before eating.

PREPARATION TIME
30 minutes

COOKING TIME
10 minutes

SERVES
2

The special thing about this stir-fried noodle dish, which is influenced by Chinese cuisine, is that the noodles are marinated with black soy sauce and pan-fried a little until they're slightly charred on the outside, before being fried with the sauce and other ingredients. When everything is cooked quickly together over high heat, a chemical reaction occurs, giving the noodles a unique fragrance and slightly smoky taste. Called the Maillard reaction, this is also the principle of the Cantonese cooking technique 'wok hei', which translates to 'breath of the wok'.

ผัดซีอิ๊ว

PAD SEE EW (STIR-FRIED NOODLES WITH CHINESE BROCCOLI)

- 400 g (14 oz) fresh flat rice noodles (sen yai), or 200 g (7 oz) dried rice noodles (width 1 cm/½ in)
- 2 tablespoons black soy sauce
- 400 g (14 oz) tender or semi-firm tofu, sliced
- 60 ml (2 fl oz/¼ cup) light soy sauce
- ½ teaspoon ground white pepper
- 1 tablespoon Golden Mountain seasoning sauce
- 1 tablespoon vegan oyster sauce
- 1 teaspoon sugar
- 90 ml (3 fl oz) canola (rapeseed) oil
- 200 g (7 oz) gai lan (Chinese broccoli), cut into 3 cm (1¼ in) lengths, leaves separated from stems
- 3 garlic cloves, chopped
- 2 tablespoons chilli flakes

If you're using dried noodles, soak in lukewarm water for 30 minutes, then drain. Skip this step if you're using fresh noodles.

Meanwhile, mix the tofu with 2 tablespoons of light soy sauce and white pepper and set aside to marinate for 30 minutes.

Mix the noodles with the black soy sauce.

Mix remaining light soy sauce, the Golden Mountain seasoning sauce, vegan oyster sauce and sugar in a bowl.

Heat a wok over high heat and, once hot, add half the oil and the marinated tofu. Pan-fry until both sides are slightly brown and crispy then remove from the wok.

Add remaining oil to the wok with gai lan stems and garlic and cook, stirring, for 30 seconds. Add the noodles and stir for 1–2 minutes until the noodles are slightly charred on the outside. Add the sauce and pan-fried tofu, then mix everything. Keep tossing and stirring for about 2–3 minutes, being careful not to break the noodles.

Add gai lan leaves and stir for 1 minute or until the leaves are slightly wilted. Serve the noodles with chilli flakes on the side.

PREPARATION TIME
30 minutes

COOKING TIME
10 minutes

SERVES
2

This is another spicy favourite at night markets, food stands and local restaurants across Thailand, and at many Thai restaurants around the world. Given its name, you might assume that alcohol is used when frying the noodles, but that's not the case. The sauces used for pad kee mao are similar to the ones used in its sister dish, pad see ew. Pad kee mao is called drunken noodles because 'kee mao' means 'drunkard' in Thai.

Flat rice noodles are often used here, but wheat noodles such as instant noodles will also work. Kaprao (holy basil) adds a distinct aroma.

ผัดขี้เมา
PAD KEE MAO (DRUNKEN NOODLES)

- 400 g (14 oz) fresh flat rice noodles, or 180 g (6½ oz) dried rice noodles (width 1 cm/½ in)
- 3 garlic cloves, chopped
- 2 fresh cayenne chillies, destemmed
- ¼ teaspoon salt
- 3 tablespoons soy sauce
- 1 tablespoon Golden Mountain seasoning sauce
- 1 tablespoon vegan oyster sauce
- 1 tablespoon Vegan fish sauce (page 18)
- 1 teaspoon sugar
- 75 ml (2½ fl oz) canola (rapeseed) oil
- 400 g (14 oz) tender or semi-firm tofu, sliced
- 50 g (1¾ oz) carrot, julienned
- 200 g (7 oz) gai lan (Chinese broccoli), cut into 3 cm (1¼ in) lengths, leaves separated from stems
- 30 g (1 oz) kaprao (Thai holy basil) leaves

If you're using dried noodles, soak in lukewarm water for 30 minutes, then drain. Skip this step if you're using fresh noodles.

Using a mortar and pestle, combine garlic, cayenne chillies and salt and pound the ingredients until they are all smacked.

Mix the soy sauce, Golden Mountain seasoning sauce, vegan oyster sauce, vegan fish sauce and sugar in a bowl.

Heat a wok or non-stick frying pan over medium–high heat and, once hot, add 3 tablespoons of the oil and the tofu. Cook the tofu until both sides are slightly brown and crispy then remove from pan.

Increase heat to high and add remaining oil. Add the smacked garlic and chilli and stir with chopsticks until aromatic. Add carrot and gai lan stems, stir for 1 minute, then add the rice noodles and stir for 1–2 minutes, until the noodles are slightly cooked. Add the sauce mixture and pan-fried tofu, and mix quickly so that the ingredients are covered evenly with the sauce. Keep tossing and stirring for 2–3 minutes, being careful not to break the noodles.

When the noodles are cooked, add gai lan leaves and basil, and stir for another 30 seconds to 1 minute before serving.

PREPARATION TIME
30 minutes

COOKING TIME
10 minutes

SERVES
2

'Mama' is Thailand's national brand of instant noodles. Many street vendors sell Mama noodles mixed with different seasonings. In Bangkok, there's even a small restaurant famous for its Mama noodles tom yum that is recommended by the *Michelin Guide*.

Despite the fact that they may be labelled as 'chicken flavour' or 'beef flavour', many kinds of Mama noodles are vegan. For this recipe, my version of Thailand's beloved sour and spicy soup, you can use any flavour. Most store-bought tom yum pastes are vegan, but some may contain shrimp paste or fish sauce, so check the label before you buy. Tofu puffs are generally available in supermarkets but if you can't find them, try an Asian store.

บะหมี่มาม่าต้มยำ
BA MII MAMA TOM YUM (MAMA NOODLES TOM YUM)

- 3 king oyster mushrooms
- 75 ml (2½ fl oz) canola (rapeseed) oil
- 2 garlic cloves, chopped
- 2 lemongrass stalks, smacked and sliced
- 30 g (1 oz) galangal, sliced
- 10 makrut lime leaves
- 6 birdseye chillies, destemmed and roughly chopped
- 100 g (3½ oz) tom yum paste
- 800 ml (27 fl oz) coconut cream
- 400 ml (13½ fl oz) vegetable stock
- 4 × 60 g (2 oz) packs vegan Mama noodles (any flavour)
- 20 tofu puffs
- 2 spring onions (scallions), sliced
- 1 lime, halved

Slice the mushrooms horizontally into pieces about 2 cm (¾ in) thick (separating the stems from the caps), then make some decorative cuts on each slice. Heat a non-stick pan over high heat, add 3 tablespoons of the oil and the sliced mushroom, and pan-fry until mushroom slices are browned on both sides.

Heat a wok over a medium–high heat and, once hot, add the remaining oil, the garlic, lemongrass, galangal, lime leaves and chilli, and stir until aromatic.

Add tom yum paste, stir for 30 seconds, then add the coconut cream and vegetable stock and bring to the boil. Add the seasonings from the noodle packets, then add the tofu puffs and cook for 5 minutes.

Add the noodles and cook until al dente. Use tongs to divide the noodles between two serving bowls. Pour over the soup and garnish with spring onion and lime.

PREPARATION TIME
30 minutes

COOKING TIME
30 minutes

MAKES
6 small bowls

Sold on little boats at the water markets along Bangkok's canals, these noodles are known for their rich broth and various toppings. They're cooked on a stove in the middle of the vendor's boat and served in a soup or with a red bean curd sauce. Portions are kept small to avoid spillage.

Boat noodles are extremely cheap and versatile. Since the portions are small, you can order and try multiple toppings at once. This recipe makes six small bowls with three different toppings, some of which require a little preparation in advance.

ก๋วยเตี๋ยวเรือ
KUAI TIAO RUEA (BOAT NOODLES)

BROTH

- 1 litre (34 fl oz/4 cups) vegetable stock
- 3 garlic cloves, sliced
- 30 g (1 oz) galangal, sliced
- 1 onion, sliced
- 1 celery stalk, sliced
- 2 lemongrass stalks, smacked and sliced
- 2 pandan leaves
- 5 coriander (cilantro) sprigs, cut in half to separate the roots and stems from the leaves
- 1 teaspoon coriander seeds
- 3 bay leaves
- 1 cinnamon stick
- 1 star anise
- 10 cloves
- 1 tablespoon whole white pepper
- 200 g (7 oz) daikon (white radish), sliced
- 30 g (1 oz) rock sugar
- 2 tablespoons soy sauce
- 3 tablespoons dark soy sauce
- 1 tablespoon vegan oyster sauce
- 3 tablespoons Vegan fish sauce (page 18)

To make the broth, bring the vegetable stock to the boil in a large saucepan over medium heat. Add garlic, galangal, onion, celery, lemongrass, pandan leaves, coriander roots and stems, coriander seeds, bay leaves, cinnamon stick, star anise, cloves and white pepper.

Return mixture to the boil, and add daikon, rock sugar, soy sauce, dark soy sauce, vegan oyster sauce and vegan fish sauce. Reduce heat to low, cover and cook for 30 minutes.

To make the red bean curd sauce, mix 90 ml (3 fl oz) of the broth with the red bean curd in a bowl. Smash it with a spoon, then add the soy sauce and vinegar and mix.

If you're using dried noodles, soak them first in water for 30 minutes, then drain. Bring a saucepan of water to the boil over medium heat, add the rice noodles and cook for 30 seconds to 1 minute until they are done (be careful not to overcook them). Take noodles out and divide between six small serving bowls. Return the water to the boil, add the bean sprouts and water spinach to the water for 30 seconds, then drain.

⟶

RED BEAN CURD SAUCE

- 2 tablespoons fermented red bean curd
- 2 tablespoons soy sauce
- 1 tablespoon rice vinegar

TOPPINGS

- 200 g (7 oz) dried thin rice noodles or vermicelli, or 400 g (14 oz) fresh thin rice noodles
- 60 g (2 oz) bean sprouts
- 100 g (3½ oz) water spinach stems, cut into 3 cm (1¼ in) lengths
- 6 wonton wrappers, cut diagonally and deep-fried
- 200 g (7 oz) tender or semi-firm tofu, sliced and pan-fried
- 4 fried bean curd rolls (响铃卷)
- 60 g (2¼ oz) fried garlic
- 2 spring onions (scallions), chopped
- 2 coriander (cilantro) sprigs, chopped

Divide the water spinach stems between two of the small serving bowls. Divide the pan-fried tofu and bean sprouts between two more of the bowls. In the remaining two bowls, add two fried bean curd rolls.

In each of the six bowls, add two fried wonton wrappers, 1 tablespoon of the fried garlic and 1 tablespoon of the red bean curd sauce. Pour over the broth until it barely covers the noodles, then sprinkle the spring onion and coriander sprigs on top.

PREPARATION TIME
15 minutes

COOKING TIME
30 minutes

SERVES
2

The combination of rich, creamy broth and contrasting fresh, crunchy toppings makes this famous dish a popular and comforting meal, especially on cooler evenings. Traditionally made with chicken or beef, the dish is believed to have been introduced by Chinese Muslim immigrants from Yunnan when they travelled along the spice route to Northern Thailand. This vegan version uses mushrooms and tofu puffs.

ข้าวซอย

KHAO SOI (NORTHERN THAI CURRY NOODLES)

- 360 ml (12 fl oz) canola (rapeseed) oil
- 400 ml (13½ fl oz) coconut cream
- 400 ml (13½ fl oz) vegetable stock
- 20 g (¾ oz) coconut (palm) sugar
- 3 tablespoons soy sauce
- 4 king oyster mushrooms, halved lengthways
- 300 g (10½ oz) tofu puffs
- 400 g (14 oz) fresh wheat noodles or 250 g (9 oz) dried wheat noodles
- 1 shallot, sliced
- 100 g (3½ oz) Thai pickled mustard greens (sour mustard greens), sliced
- 2 spring onions (scallions), sliced
- coriander (cilantro), to garnish
- 1 lime, cut into wedges

KHAO SOI PASTE

- 10 dried chillies, soaked in water for 5 minutes, then drained
- 6 garlic cloves
- 3 shallots, sliced
- 30 g (1 oz) fresh ginger, sliced
- 1 tablespoon coriander seeds
- 6 coriander (cilantro) roots
- 20 g (¾ oz) turmeric, sliced
- 2 lemongrass stalks, sliced
- 2 tablespoons sugar
- 3 tablespoons soybean paste

Combine all the ingredients for the khao soi paste in a food processor and blend to form a smooth paste.

Heat a wok or large non-stick frying pan over medium–high heat and, once hot, add 60 ml (2 fl oz/¼ cup) of the canola oil. Add the khao soi paste, stir for 2–3 minutes until it becomes darker and aromatic, then add coconut cream.

Bring the broth to the boil, then add the vegetable stock, coconut sugar and soy sauce. Return to the boil, add mushroom and tofu puffs and cook for 5 minutes.

Bring a separate saucepan of water to the boil and cook the noodles according to the packet instructions. Drain and set aside.

Heat the remaining oil in a large saucepan over medium–high heat. To check whether it is hot enough for deep-frying, hold a wooden chopstick in the oil. If it is immediately surrounded by tiny bubbles, the oil is ready to use. Take one-quarter of the cooked noodles and deep-fry until golden and crispy. Divide the remaining cooked noodles between two large serving bowls.

Divide the curry broth, mushroom, tofu puffs, deep-fried noodles, shallot, pickled mustard greens, spring onion and coriander between bowls. Squeeze some lime juice on top before serving.

PREPARATION TIME
20 minutes

SERVES
2

Made with green (unripe) papaya, som tam is a refreshing, tangy dish, and a staple of Thai cuisine. Unlike ripe papaya, which has a fruity flavour and a tender texture, green papaya is firm and tastes more like a gourd than a fruit.

For the salad, the green papaya is shredded into thin strips, then mixed with ingredients like chilli, garlic, green beans, lime juice, fish sauce, tomatoes and peanuts. The salad balances sweet, sour, salty and spicy flavours, creating a zesty, crunchy, colourful dish. It's often served as a side or a light meal at street stands.

ส้มตำ

SOM TAM (GREEN PAPAYA SALAD)

- 5 garlic cloves
- 3 birdseye chillies, destemmed
- 1 tablespoon coconut (palm) sugar
- 1½ teaspoons tamarind sauce
- 50 ml (1¾ fl oz) Vegan fish sauce (page 18)
- 50 ml (1¾ fl oz) lime juice
- 400 g (14 oz) green papaya, peeled and julienned
- 60 g (2 oz) long green beans (yard-long beans), cut into 3 cm (1¼ in) lengths
- 100 g (3½ oz) tomatoes, cut into wedges
- 100 g (3½ oz) roasted and salted peanuts

Using a large mortar and pestle, pound the garlic and chilli until they are well smacked.

Add coconut sugar, tamarind sauce, vegan fish sauce and lime juice and continue pounding for about 30 seconds until the ingredients are mixed.

Add papaya, beans and tomato and mix everything well. Top with peanuts to serve.

PREPARATION TIME
10 minutes

COOKING TIME
5 minutes

SERVES
2

Pad kaprao is one of the quickest and easiest Thai dishes to make, if you have the right ingredients to hand. Street vendors cook it very quickly over strong flames, then pack it in paper with rice and a fried egg to make it easy to take-away. Kaprao (Thai holy basil) gives this dish its very distinct taste and aroma. Fresh kaprao is not easy to find, but many Asian stores have frozen kaprao that, while not as good as fresh, preserves the unique character of the herb.

Traditionally made with pork mince, vegan pad kaprao can be made using vegan mince (as I have here), mushrooms or tofu.

ผัดกะเพรา

PAD KAPRAO (STIR-FRIED VEGAN MINCE WITH HOLY BASIL)

- 4 garlic cloves
- 3 birdseye chillies, destemmed
- 3 fresh cayenne chillies, destemmed
- 2 tablespoons soy sauce
- ½ tablespoon Golden Mountain seasoning sauce
- 1 tablespoon dark soy sauce
- 1 tablespoon vegan oyster sauce
- 2 tablespoons Vegan fish sauce (page 18)
- 2 teaspoons coconut (palm) sugar
- 500 g (1 lb 2 oz) vegan mince
- 75 ml (2½ fl oz) canola (rapeseed) oil
- 100 g (3½ oz) kaprao (Thai holy basil) leaves
- steamed rice, to serve

Using a pestle and mortar, pound the garlic, birdseye chillies and cayenne chillies until they are well smacked.

In a bowl or jug, mix together all the sauces and the coconut sugar.

Break the vegan mince into small pieces to allow it to cook faster.

Heat a wok over medium–high heat. Once hot, add the oil, and the smacked garlic and chilli. Stir for a minute until aromatic, then add the vegan mince and increase heat to high. Stir for 2–3 minutes until the colour darkens a little.

Pour in the sauce mixture and stir quickly until the sauce is absorbed. Add the kaprao leaves and stir for a further 30 seconds. Serve the dish with rice.

PREPARATION TIME
8 hours

COOKING TIME
20 minutes

MAKES
12

These skewers, which can be found at night markets and roadside food stands, are typically served on banana leaves with sticky rice (khao neow). 'Moo' means 'pork' and 'ping' refers to the roasting or grilling process.

I use seitan (also known as vital wheat gluten) in this vegan version and share two ways to cook the skewers: grilling over a charcoal stove (the traditional method) or pan-frying (more suitable for a home kitchen). If you can't find seitan flour in your local supermarket, you'll find it in an Asian store.

หมูปิ้งเจ
MOO PING JAY (GRILLED SEITAN SKEWERS)

- ⅔ teaspoon salt
- 120 ml (4 fl oz) coconut milk
- 200 g (7 oz) seitan (vital wheat gluten) flour
- ⅔ teaspoon whole black peppercorns
- 4 garlic cloves, finely chopped
- 5 coriander (cilantro) roots
- 60 ml (2 fl oz/¼ cup) soy sauce
- 2 tablespoons black soy sauce
- 2 tablespoons Vegan fish sauce (page 18)
- 2 tablespoons vegan oyster sauce
- 2 tablespoons coconut (palm) sugar
- 1 tablespoon tapioca flour
- 2 tablespoons sesame oil
- 3 tablespoons canola (rapeseed) oil (if pan-frying)

In a bowl, mix salt and coconut milk with 100 ml (3½ fl oz) of water. Add the seitan flour, knead the mixture into a dough, then shape into a ball. (The amount of liquid needed for the seitan flour depends on the brand. If there is still dry flour that you cannot knead into the dough after you've added the coconut milk and water, just add a bit more water.) Set aside to rest for 15 minutes.

Bring a saucepan of water to the boil, add the dough and boil for 15 minutes, then set aside to cool. Once it has cooled down, cut into large slices (about 3 cm long x 6 cm wide x 5 mm thick/1¼ in x 2½ in x ¼ in).

Using a mortar and pestle, pound black peppercorns until coarsely crushed. Add garlic and coriander roots, and pound to form a paste.

Mix the smacked mixture with soy sauce, black soy sauce, vegan fish sauce, vegan oyster sauce, coconut sugar, tapioca flour and sesame oil until all the ingredients are well combined. Coat the seitan slices evenly with the mixture and set aside to marinate for at least 6 hours, preferably overnight, in the fridge.

Push the marinated seitan slices onto barbecue skewers.

Chargrill until slightly charred. Alternatively, heat a non-stick frying pan over medium heat and, once hot, add the canola oil. Add the seitan skewers and pan-fry until both sides are slightly charred and crispy.

PREPARATION TIME
15 minutes

COOKING TIME
30 minutes

SERVES
4

Tom kha is a creamy, aromatic Thai soup known for its signature balance of sour, spicy and subtly sweet flavours. Traditionally made with coconut milk and infused with fresh herbs like galangal and makrut lime leaves, the dish is also called tom kha gai - with 'tom' meaning 'to boil' or 'soup', 'kha' referring to galangal, and 'gai' meaning chicken in Thai. In my vegan version, I swap the chicken for mushrooms and tofu.

While tom kha is a popular staple in Thai restaurants, it's also commonly found at street markets, especially among vendors specialising in curries and soups. Typically served with rice, tom kha is a comforting, nourishing dish that's both hearty and bursting with flavour.

ต้มข่า
TOM KHA (COCONUT GALANGAL SOUP)

- 3 tablespoons canola (rapeseed) oil
- 4 garlic cloves, sliced
- 3 lemongrass stalks, smacked and sliced
- 3 shallots, sliced
- 30 g (1 oz) galangal, smacked and sliced
- 10 makrut lime leaves
- 6 dried chillies
- 4 king oyster mushrooms, sliced
- 10 white or brown button mushrooms, sliced
- 600 ml (20½ fl oz) coconut cream
- 600 ml (20½ fl oz) vegetable stock
- 60 ml (¼ cup/2 fl oz) tamarind sauce
- 3 tablespoons Vegan fish sauce (page 18)
- 1½ tablespoons coconut (palm) sugar
- salt, to taste
- 10 tofu puffs, halved
- 2 birdseye chillies, destemmed and sliced
- 100 g (3½ oz) tomatoes, cut into wedges, or 6 cherry tomatoes, halved
- 50 ml (1¾ fl oz) lime juice

Heat a large saucepan over medium heat and, once hot, add oil, garlic, lemongrass, shallot, galangal, lime leaves and dried chillies. Stir for 1 minute until aromatic, then add all the mushroom and stir for another minute.

Add coconut cream and bring to the boil. Add vegetable stock, tamarind sauce, vegan fish sauce, coconut sugar and salt to taste.

Add tofu puffs and cook for 15 minutes over low–medium heat before adding the birdseye chillies and tomato. Cook for a further 2 minutes, then add the lime juice and serve.

PREPARATION TIME
5 minutes

COOKING TIME
10 minutes

SERVES
2

Fried bananas or plantains feature in many cuisines and the Thai version is a classic street food snack. Slices of banana are coated in a thick batter, then deep-fried. Often eaten on the go, they are best enjoyed when they're warm and crunchy, and are an example of how street food can take a simple ingredient and transform it into something unforgettable.

Nam wah bananas (also known as Thai bananas) are shorter, firmer and not as sweet as the widely available Cavendish variety. They also keep their shape well during frying. If you can't get nam wah, use plantains (cooking bananas) or semi-ripe Cavendish bananas instead (ripe bananas will go squashy when deep-fried).

กล้วยทอด
KLUAY TOD (BANANA FRITTERS)

- 100 g (3½ oz) rice flour
- 2 tablespoons cornflour (cornstarch)
- 50 g (1¾ oz) finely grated unsweetened coconut flakes
- 30 g (1 oz) sugar
- ½ teaspoon salt
- 30 g (1 oz) white sesame seeds
- 2 teaspoons bicarbonate of soda (baking soda)
- 200 ml (7 fl oz) coconut milk
- 800 ml (27 fl oz) canola (rapeseed) oil
- 500 g (1 lb 2 oz) bananas (nam wah or semi-ripe Cavendish) or plantains, peeled and sliced lengthways into 5 mm (¼ in) slices

Mix rice flour, cornflour, coconut flakes, sugar, salt and sesame seeds in a large bowl. In another bowl, mix the bicarb soda and coconut milk, then pour the liquid into the large bowl with the flour mixture and mix everything into a smooth batter with no lumps.

Heat the oil in a large saucepan over medium–high heat. To check whether it is hot enough for deep-frying, hold a wooden chopstick in the oil. If it is immediately surrounded by tiny bubbles, the oil is ready to use. Keep the oil temperature steady for deep-frying.

Dip the banana slices in the batter, turning them so they are evenly coated, then deep-fry for 8–10 minutes until golden and crispy. Remove and place on a serving dish. Serve immediately.

PREPARATION TIME
10 minutes, plus 2 hours chilling

COOKING TIME
25 minutes

MAKES
8

This traditional two-layered Thai dessert, with delicate texture and subtle flavour, is often served by street vendors and restaurants as a refreshing snack after a meal. The bottom layer is made with coconut milk, starch and water chestnuts, taro or corn. The top layer is creamy and typically made with coconut milk and pandan leaves, providing a unique fragrance and contrasting texture.

For this recipe, I use small sago (tapioca) pearls for the bottom layer because they are readily available and their distinct sensation makes the dessert fun to eat. In the photograph, the pudding is served in banana-leaf cups, but muffin cases or moulds make an easy substitute.

ขนมตะโก้

KHANOM TAKO (COCONUT PUDDING)

- 50 g (1¾ oz) small sago (tapioca) pearls (preferably pandan flavour)
- 2 tablespoons sugar
- 200 ml (7 fl oz) coconut milk
- 3 pandan leaves
- 1 tablespoon cornflour (cornstarch)
- 1 tablespoon sweetcorn kernels

Bring 500 ml (17 fl oz/2 cups) of water to the boil in a saucepan over medium heat. Add the sago pearls and cook for 10 minutes, stirring. Turn off heat and cover, then set aside for 15 minutes (the residual heat will cook the sago a little further).

Drain and rinse the sago, then transfer to a bowl and mix with 1 tablespoon of the sugar. Half-fill each of 8 muffin cases or moulds with the cooked sago pearls.

Heat the coconut milk, pandan leaves and remaining sugar in a saucepan over medium heat. Bring to the boil then reduce heat to low and discard the pandan leaves.

Mix the cornflour with 40 ml (1¼ fl oz) of water and pour it into the saucepan. Mix for about 30 seconds until the texture thickens, then divide the mixture between the 8 cases or moulds. Place a piece of corn in the middle of each portion. Chill in the fridge for 2 hours before serving.

PREPARATION TIME
2 hours

COOKING TIME
30 minutes

MAKES
14 portions (using an æbleskiver pan) or 20 portions (using a takoyaki pan)

Loved for their rich flavour and delightful texture, these bite-sized pancakes, with either savoury or sweet toppings, are cooked in a special cast-iron pan with round indentations, similar to a Japanese takoyaki pan or a Danish æbleskiver pan. If you don't have a pan like this, you can also make a flat pancake with this batter. It's important to use a non-stick pan brushed with oil for maximum crunch and to prevent sticking.

At street food markets, the aroma of the sizzling coconut batter is always a drawcard! Served straight off the griddle, khanom krok are easy to eat on the go, while they're still warm and crispy.

ขนมครก

KHANOM KROK (COCONUT RICE PANCAKES)

- 2 tablespoons coconut oil, melted
- 1 spring onion (scallion), sliced
- 1 tablespoon sweetcorn kernels
- 1 teaspoon toasted black sesame seeds

BOTTOM-LAYER BATTER

- 100 ml (3½ fl oz) coconut cream
- 30 g (1 oz) rice flour
- 50 g (1¾ oz) cooked jasmine rice
- 2 teaspoons grated coconut flakes
- 1 tablespoon coconut (palm) sugar
- ¼ teaspoon salt

TOP-LAYER BATTER

- 70 ml (2¼ fl oz) coconut cream
- 1 tablespoon rice flour
- 2 teaspoons sugar
- small pinch of salt

To make the bottom-layer batter, mix all the ingredients plus 50 ml (1¾ fl oz) of water with an electric mixer until smooth. In another bowl, mix everything for the top-layer batter plus 30 ml (1 fl oz) of water until smooth.

Heat a takoyaki or Æbleskiver pan over low–medium heat and brush each hole with coconut oil. Pour in the bottom-layer batter until each hole is two-thirds full, then heat until the surface of the batter is a little cooked (no longer completely liquid). Pour the top-layer batter into each hole until full and cook for 1–2 minutes.

Cover and cook for about 5 minutes until a skewer inserted into the middle of one hole comes out clean and the base of each pancake is brown and crisp. Remove from pan and sprinkle with spring onion, corn and sesame seeds to serve.

PREPARATION TIME
4 hours

COOKING TIME
30 minutes

SERVES
2

Throughout Thailand, you'll find stands loaded with fresh mangoes and khao niew mamuang in transparent takeaway boxes. The rice is often multicoloured because the vendors dye it with fruits or food pigment to make it look extra appealing.

A key flavour in this dessert is pandan, a tropical plant with long, fragrant green leaves. Commonly used in Southeast Asian cuisine for both flavour and natural colouring, pandan adds a distinctive aroma and delicious taste. While fresh leaves can be tricky to find, many Asian stores carry them frozen. Alternatively, pandan extract is a great substitute.

- 200 g (7 oz) glutinous rice
- 6 pandan leaves or 2 tablespoons pandan extract
- 300 ml (10 fl oz) Thai coconut cream
- 40 g (1½ oz) coconut (palm) sugar
- small pinch of salt
- 1 tablespoon cornflour (cornstarch)
- 1 ripe mango, peeled and sliced
- extra pandan leaf (optional), to garnish

ข้าวเหนียวมะม่วง

KHAO NIEW MAMUANG (MANGO STICKY RICE)

Soak the glutinous rice in water for 4 hours. Drain the water, put 3 of the pandan leaves in a steamer (preferably bamboo) and pour the rice on top. (If you don't have pandan leaves, mix the rice with 1 tablespoon of pandan extract instead.) Steam the rice for about 25 minutes over medium–high heat until cooked. Transfer to a bowl.

Meanwhile, heat a pot over medium heat. Add the coconut cream, coconut sugar, salt and remaining pandan leaves (or 1 tablespoon of pandan extract). Cook for 1–2 minutes, stirring, until the sauce starts to bubble up. Remove and discard the pandan leaves, if using.

Pour half of the sauce over the rice and mix well. Transfer to a serving dish.

To make the topping, mix the cornflour with 2 tablespoons of water and add to the remaining sauce in the pot. Mix everything well, cook for 1 minute, then turn off the heat. Pour the topping sauce from the pot over the rice. Garnish with a small piece of fresh pandan leaf, if desired. Serve alongside the mango.

PREPARATION TIME
5 minutes, plus 20 minutes cooling

COOKING TIME
10 minutes

MAKES
2 glasses, each 500 ml (17 fl oz/2 cups)

Cha yen is Thailand's most popular drink. You'll find stands and shops selling all sorts of varieties, with or without milk. Here, I am sharing the most common, which is made with a mix of black and green Thai tea, combined with plant-based condensed milk and plant-based milk.

This drink is super refreshing, smooth and tasty – ideal for a hot summer's day.

ชาเย็น
CHA YEN (ICED TEA)

- 20 g (¾ oz) Thai black and green tea mix
- 40 g (1½ oz) sugar
- 300 g (10½ oz) ice cubes
- 50 ml (1¾ fl oz) Coconut condensed milk (page 28)
- 300 ml (10 fl oz) plant-based milk

Add the Thai tea mix to a tea strainer or bag. Bring 600 ml (20½ fl oz) of water to the boil in a small saucepan over low–medium heat, add the tea strainer or bag and simmer for 10 minutes before removing it.

To 'pull' the tea, pour it from the saucepan into another pot in a thin, steady stream, creating some distance between the two vessels (the saucepan should be at least 50 centimetres or 20 inches higher than the pot – the higher the better). Then, switch the vessels, holding the pot above, and pour the tea back into the saucepan. Repeat this process four times to integrate more air into the tea, making it taste richer and smoother.

Add sugar, stir well and leave the tea to cool for about 20 minutes.

Divide the ice cubes, condensed milk, tea and the plant-based milk between two glasses and mix well before drinking.

VIETNAM

Street food is deeply rooted in Vietnam's rich culinary history. When the traditions of Vietnamese and French cuisine collided in the nineteenth and twentieth centuries, a new food culture was formed and many delicacies were created. They include Vietnamese versions of the baguette sandwich (bánh mì, page 122), iced coffee (cà phê sữa dá, page 126) and crème caramel (bánh flan). You can experience the authentic taste of different regions at the street markets and roadside stalls of major cities as well as smaller towns.

The preparation of street foods varies between regions, particularly between the North and the South. For example, when it comes to the beloved phở (page 114), the Northern phở (phở bắc or phở hà nội) has a lighter, clearer broth and fewer toppings, while the Southern phở (phở Sài Gòn) tends to be sweeter and comes with more toppings.

As a country with vast rice fields, rice is at the heart of Vietnamese street food – from rice noodles to chả giò/nem rán (fried spring rolls, page 110) and gỏi cuốn (summer rolls wrapped with rice paper, page 113) to bánh cuốn (steamed rice rolls, page 118) and bánh xèo (savoury pancakes made with rice flour). Many of the dishes are quite light and refreshing, and meat and seafood are often served with fresh herbs and vegetables, which help to balance out any heaviness. Herbs such as mint, Thai basil, coriander (cilantro) and Vietnamese coriander (also called Vietnamese mint or laksa leaves) are commonly used, enhancing the aroma, taste and freshness of the food. Fish sauce, soy sauce, lime and chilli are the base of many dishes, adding depth and an extra kick to the flavours. By swapping out the meat or seafood for plant-based proteins and using vegan fish sauce (page 18), many Vietnamese street foods can be easily made vegan.

Night markets and roadside stalls are not to be missed when visiting Vietnam. In Hanoi, the Old Quarter is renowned for its Northern delicacies, while the Ben Thanh Market in Ho Chi Minh City offers a wide variety of Southern specialities, including hủ tiếu (a popular noodle soup eaten for breakfast).

PREPARATION TIME
40 minutes

COOKING TIME
20 minutes

MAKES
12

The possible variations on spring rolls are endless. Traditionally filled with ground pork (I use vegan mince instead), vermicelli and a few vegetables (most commonly carrot), the ingredients are chopped or diced, simply seasoned, then wrapped in rice paper and deep-fried.

Spring rolls are often served with fresh lettuce or herbs and nước chấm for dipping. Although they are a popular street food in their own right, they are also an important component of many Vietnamese dishes, including bún thịt nướng chả giò, a popular cold vermicelli dish (see the vegan version on page 116).

CHẢ GIÒ/NEM RÁN
FRIED SPRING ROLLS

- 6 g (⅛ oz) dried black fungus (wood ear mushrooms)
- 160 g (5½ oz) vegan mince
- 80 g (2¾ oz) carrot, shredded
- 30 g (1 oz) vermicelli rice noodles, soaked in hot water for 5 minutes, then drained and chopped
- 30 g (1 oz) red onion, chopped
- 1 tablespoon Vegan fish sauce (page 18)
- 1 tablespoon vegan oyster sauce
- 1½ tablespoons soy sauce
- 1 tablespoon sesame oil
- ½ teaspoon ground white pepper
- ½ teaspoon sugar
- ¼ teaspoon salt
- 12 rice paper rounds (diameter 26 cm/10¼ in)
- 600 ml (20½ fl oz) canola (rapeseed) oil
- 120 ml (4 fl oz) Nước chấm (page 20)

Soak the dried black fungus in warm water for 15 minutes, then drain and chop.

Mix the fungus, vegan mince, carrot, chopped vermicelli, onion, vegan fish sauce, vegan oyster sauce, soy sauce, sesame oil, white pepper, sugar and salt in a large bowl. Mix everything well and set aside to marinate for 15 minutes.

Fill a large, shallow bowl (bigger than the rice paper rounds) with water. Working one at a time, place a rice paper round in the water for 15 seconds, then remove onto a flat surface.

Fold the bottom side of the rice paper up about 2 cm (¾ in) from the edge to create a double-layered area for the filling. Spoon about 2 tablespoons of the filling onto this area. Then fold the left and right sides of the rice paper in so that the two ends of the filling are covered. Holding the filling, roll the rice paper until it becomes a tight wrap. Repeat with remaining rounds and filling.

Heat the oil in a large saucepan over medium–high heat until the oil reaches 160°C–170°C (320°–340°F) on a kitchen thermometer. (If you don't have a thermometer, hold a wooden chopstick in the oil; if it is immediately surrounded by tiny bubbles, the oil is ready to use.) Working in batches, use chopsticks to add the spring rolls to the oil one after another. Keep separating them while frying so they don't stick together. Deep-fry until the spring rolls are golden, crispy and bubbly on the outside, then remove and place on a serving dish.

Cut the spring rolls in half and serve with nước chấm.

PREPARATION TIME
30 minutes

MAKES
10

Refreshing, delicious, easy to prepare and requiring no cooking, gỏi cuốn is the ideal summer food. This dish also features a peanut sauce that makes a delicious dip for many other snacks. The chilli garlic sauce used in the peanut sauce can be found in Asian stores.

At markets and street stalls, gỏi cuốn is prepared to order, with all the fresh ingredients laid out on the counter, allowing customers to pick their favourite combinations.

GỎI CUỐN
SUMMER ROLLS

- 60 g (2 oz) dried vermicelli
- 3 tablespoons canola (rapeseed) oil
- 500 g (1 lb 2 oz) tender or semi-firm tofu, sliced about ½ cm (¼ in) thick
- 10 rice paper rounds (diameter 26 cm/10¼ in or 28 cm/11 in)
- 100 g (3½ oz) carrot, julienned
- 80 g (2¾ oz) bean sprouts
- 150 g (5½ oz) cucumber, julienned
- 50 g (1¾ oz) lettuce, julienned
- 2 avocados, sliced
- 1 mango, peeled and julienned
- coriander (cilantro) sprig, chopped
- 100 ml (3½ fl oz) Nước chấm (page 20), for dipping

PEANUT SAUCE

- 60 ml (2 fl oz/¼ cup) hoisin sauce
- 2 tablespoons peanut butter
- 2 teaspoons Vietnamese chilli garlic sauce
- 1 tablespoon Vegan fish sauce (page 18)
- 1 teaspoon lime juice
- 2 tablespoons roasted and salted peanuts, crushed

Combine 2 tablespoons of water with all the ingredients for the peanut sauce, except the peanuts. Sprinkle crushed peanuts on top. Set aside.

Cook the vermicelli according to packet instructions, then soak in cold water.

Heat a wok or non-stick frying pan over medium–high heat and, once hot, add the oil and the tofu. Fry the tofu on both sides until slightly brown and crispy, then remove from the pan.

Fill a large, shallow bowl with water. Working one at a time, place a rice paper round in the water for 15 seconds, then remove and place on a plate.

Add a little carrot, bean sprouts, cucumber, lettuce, vermicelli, fried tofu, avocado, mango and coriander to the bottom third of the rice paper round, about 2 cm (¾ in) from the edge. (If you want an ingredient to be clearly visible in the roll, such as avocado or mango, place that ingredient first on the rice paper.)

Take the bottom edge of the rice paper round and fold it up, then fold in the left and right sides to enclose the filling. Press the ingredients together with your fingers and roll up the rice paper carefully. Repeat with remaining rice paper rounds and filling.

Serve with the peanut sauce and nước chấm.

PREPARATION TIME
1 hour

COOKING TIME
30 minutes

SERVES
2

Phở is one of the most well-known Vietnamese street foods. The broth is light and aromatic, simmered for hours with a combination of spices to give a deep, savoury flavour, and topped with fresh herbs and condiments. Every vendor has their own family recipe that makes their broth unique.

PHỞ
RICE NOODLE SOUP

- 6 dried shiitake mushrooms
- 400 g (14 oz) fresh flat rice noodles (hor fun) or 200 g (7 oz) dried rice noodles
- 90 ml (3 fl oz/6 tablespoons) canola (rapeseed) oil
- 300 g (11 oz) tender or semi-firm tofu, diced
- 1 lemongrass stalk, sliced
- 1 onion, quartered
- 40 g (1½ oz) fresh ginger, sliced
- 2 shallots, halved
- 1 cinnamon stick
- 5 bay leaves
- 2 star anise
- 1 nutmeg
- 1 teaspoon ground black pepper
- 1 teaspoon whole cloves
- 1 teaspoon fennel seeds
- 1 litre (34 fl oz/4 cups) vegetable stock
- 200 g (7 oz) daikon (white radish), sliced 1.5 cm (½ in) thick
- 100 g (3½ oz) carrot, chopped
- 60 ml (2 fl oz/¼ cup) Vegan fish sauce (page 18)
- 20 g (¾ oz) rock sugar
- 2 king oyster mushrooms, sliced lengthways
- 100 g (3½ oz) bean sprouts
- 2 spring onions (scallions)
- 2 coriander (cilantro) sprigs
- 2 Thai basil sprigs, sliced
- 2 birdseye chillies, destemmed
- 2 lime wedges

Soak the shiitake mushrooms for 1 hour. If you're using dried rice noodles, soak in lukewarm water for 30 minutes, then drain. Skip this step if you're using fresh rice noodles.

Heat a wok or non-stick frying pan over medium–high heat and, once hot, add half the oil and the tofu. Fry the tofu on all sides until slightly brown and crispy, then remove from the pan.

Wipe out the pan then add the lemongrass, onion, ginger and shallot and cook for a few minutes, turning, until slightly charred. Remove from pan.

Add the cinnamon stick, bay leaves, star anise, nutmeg, black pepper, cloves and fennel seeds to the pan and toast for a few minutes, tossing, until aromatic. Be careful not to burn the spices. Put the toasted spices in a muslin (cheesecloth) or cotton bag and seal.

Bring the vegetable stock to the boil in a large saucepan over high heat. Add the shiitake mushrooms, lemongrass mixture, daikon, carrot and spice bag. Reduce heat to low and simmer for 15 minutes.

Meanwhile, chop the spring onions, coriander sprigs, Thai basil sprigs and birdseye chillies.

To the simmering stock, add vegan fish sauce, rock sugar and fried tofu. Season to taste with salt and cook for a further 10 minutes. Discard the spice bag.

Meanwhile, reheat the wok or frying pan over medium–high heat and, once hot, add the remaining oil. Pan-fry the king oyster mushroom slices until both sides are golden. Remove from pan.

Add the noodles to the broth and cook for 1–2 minutes until al dente, taking care not to overcook. Divide the noodles and broth mixture between two large serving bowls. Top each bowl with the pan-fried king oyster mushroom slices, bean sprouts, spring onion, coriander, Thai basil, birdseye chilli and lime.

PREPARATION TIME
3 hours

COOKING TIME
15 minutes

SERVES
2

- 400 g (14 oz) oyster mushrooms
- 100 g (3½ oz) carrots, julienned
- 100 g (3½ oz) daikon (white radish), julienned
- ½ teaspoon salt
- 90 ml (3 fl oz) rice vinegar
- 2 tablespoons sugar
- 150 g (5½ oz) dried rice vermicelli
- 3 tablespoons canola (rapeseed) oil (if pan-frying)
- 50 g (1¾ oz) lettuce leaves
- 150 g (5½ oz) cucumber
- 2 mint sprigs
- 4 Chả giò/Nem rán (Fried spring rolls, page 110), halved
- 60 g (2 oz) roasted and salted peanuts, roughly chopped
- 2 fresh cayenne chillies, destemmed and sliced
- 100 ml (3½ fl oz) Nước chấm (page 20)

MUSHROOM MARINADE

- 3 garlic cloves
- 50 g (1¾ oz) onion
- 1 lemongrass stalk
- 2 tablespoons Vegan fish sauce (page 18)
- 2 tablespoons soy sauce
- 2 tablespoons vegan oyster sauce
- 2 tablespoons sesame oil
- 1 teaspoon sugar
- ½ teaspoon ground white pepper
- 1 teaspoon Chinese five-spice

Street vendors will prepare this cold vermicelli dish while you wait. It is traditionally served with pork, but I use oyster mushrooms instead, which have a meaty texture and a slightly smoky flavour after being marinated and grilled or fried.

BÚN 'THỊT' NƯỚNG CHẢ GIÒ

RICE VERMICELLI WITH VEGAN GRILLED 'MEAT' AND SPRING ROLLS

To make the mushroom marinade, finely shop the garlic cloves, onion and lemongrass stalk, and mix all the marinade ingredients together in a bowl.

Add the oyster mushrooms to the marinade and set aside to marinate for 3 hours.

Meanwhile, combine carrot, daikon and salt in a bowl or jar; mix and set aside to rest for 15 minutes. Drain any excess water from the vegetables. Add vinegar, 200 ml (7 fl oz) of water and the sugar, then cover and set aside to pickle for 2 hours. Drain the liquid.

Soak the vermicelli in water for 30 minutes, then drain.

Remove the oyster mushrooms from the mushroom marinade and chargrill or cook in an air-fryer (at 200°C/390°F) for 12 minutes, until browned and slightly charred on the outside. Alternatively, heat the canola oil in a non-stick frying pan over high heat, add mushrooms and cook until slightly charred on both sides.

Cook the soaked, drained noodles according to packet instructions, then drain.

Shred the lettuce leaves and julienne the cucumber.

Divide the noodles, pickled carrot and daikon, lettuce, cucumber, mint, oyster mushrooms, chả giò/nem rán (fried spring rolls) and peanuts between two serving bowls. Garnish with sliced chilli, according to taste.

Before eating, pour the nước chấm over the vermicelli and vegetables and mix well.

PREPARATION TIME
15 minutes

COOKING TIME
30 minutes

SERVES
2

Light yet satisfying, and typically eaten for breakfast, steamed rice rolls are a well-known street food, not only in Vietnam, but also in China. Ground pork and dried black fungus (wood ear mushrooms) are the classic filling, but you can use anything you like – I use vegan mince instead of pork.

Traditionally, the rice batter is made from rice and water, and is poured on a piece of cloth stretched over a pot of boiling water to steam. Here, I use an easier method where the batter is poured onto a plate steamed in a pot.

BÁNH CUỐN
STEAMED RICE ROLLS

- 3 tablespoons canola (rapeseed) oil, plus extra for greasing
- 60 g (2 oz) onion, chopped
- 300 g (10½ oz) vegan mince
- 10 g (¼ oz) dried black fungus (wood ear mushrooms), soaked in warm water for 15 minutes, then drained and chopped
- 2 tablespoons Vegan fish sauce (page 18)
- 2 tablespoons soy sauce
- 1 tablespoon sesame oil
- 1 teaspoon sugar
- ½ teaspoon ground white pepper
- 160 g (5½ oz) rice flour
- 40 g (1½ oz) tapioca flour
- 2 tablespoons crisp fried shallots or fried onion
- 100 ml (3½ fl oz) Nước chấm (page 20)

Heat a wok or frying pan over medium–high heat and, once hot, add oil, onion and vegan mince, breaking up the mince with a spatula. Cook for 2–3 minutes until the colour of the vegan mince changes, then add the dried black fungus.

Add vegan fish sauce, soy sauce, sesame oil, sugar and pepper, and cook, stirring, for 1–2 minutes.

In a large bowl, mix the rice flour and tapioca flour with 400 ml (13½ fl oz) of water.

Brush a little extra oil over a flat heatproof plate (preferably stainless steel, but any flat plate will do).

Fill a saucepan with hot water and place a steam rack in the pan (the water level should not be higher than the steam rack).

Place the prepared plate on top of the steam rack, cover and steam over high heat for 30 seconds, then take the plate out with a plate holder, mix the batter again and pour a thin layer onto the plate. (The plate needs to be hot so that the rice noodle sheet doesn't crack while steaming.)

Place the plate back on the steam rack, cover and steam for 2–3 minutes (the exact time will depend on how thick the layer is and how thick the plate is).

When the noodle sheet has become completely translucent and you can see big bubbles forming under it, take out the plate. Fill a large bowl or container with cold water and float the plate in the water to cool it down. Once cool, remove the noodle sheet and carefully lay it on a flat surface. Place one scoop of the filling on the rice sheet and roll up gently. Repeat with the remaining batter and filling.

Sprinkle the fried shallots on the bánh cuốn and serve with nước chấm.

PREPARATION TIME
3 hours

COOKING TIME
15 minutes

SERVES
2

Bánh hỏi refers to both a special kind of vermicelli (where the noodles are extra thin and woven intricately together to form small rectangular noodle sheets) and the dish made from these noodles.

This form of vermicelli is loved for its light and airy texture. It's normally served with grilled meats, lettuce, fresh herbs such as mint and coriander, and, of course nước chấm. Often enjoyed at home, you can also purchase this dish, with various toppings, at food stalls and small eateries. Here, I use oyster mushrooms as a meat substitute.

BÁNH HOI 'THIT' QUAY

FINE RICE VERMICELLI WITH VEGAN ROAST 'MEAT'

MUSHROOM MARINADE

- 3 garlic cloves, finely chopped
- 50 g (1¾ oz) onion, finely chopped
- 1 lemongrass stalk, finely chopped
- 2 tablespoons Vegan fish sauce (page 18)
- 2 tablespoons soy sauce
- 2 tablespoons vegan oyster sauce
- 2 tablespoons sesame oil
- 1 teaspoon sugar
- ½ teaspoon ground white pepper
- 1 teaspoon Chinese five-spice

TOPPINGS

- 400 g (14 oz) oyster mushrooms
- 3 tablespoons canola (rapeseed) oil, plus 3 tablespoons extra (if pan-frying)
- 2 spring onions (scallions), chopped
- 200 g (7 oz) dried bánh hỏi vermicelli
- 50 g (1¾ oz) lettuce leaves, sliced
- 150 g (5½ oz) cucumber, sliced
- 2 mint sprigs
- 2 tablespoons crisp fried shallots or fried onion
- 100 ml (3½ fl oz) Nước chấm (page 20)

Mix all the mushroom marinade ingredients together in a bowl, add the oyster mushrooms and set aside to marinate for 3 hours.

Remove the oyster mushrooms from the mushroom marinade and chargrill or cook in an air-fryer (at 200°C/390°F) for 12 minutes, until browned and slightly charred on the outside. Alternatively, heat the extra canola oil in a non-stick frying pan over high heat, add mushrooms and cook until slightly charred on both sides.

Place spring onion in a small bowl. Heat the oil in a small saucepan over high heat until very hot (around 180°C/360°F), then pour it over the spring onion. Set aside.

Soak the bánh hỏi vermicelli sheets in water for 15 minutes, then drain and steam according to packet instructions.

Roll up each vermicelli sheet. Divide the vermicelli rolls, lettuce, cucumber, mint and oyster mushrooms between two serving plates and top with the spring onion in oil and the fried shallots.

Serve each plate with its own small bowl of nước chấm. Pour the nước chấm over the vermicelli and vegetables, and mix well before eating.

PREPARATION TIME
2 hours 30 minutes

COOKING TIME
30 minutes

MAKES
2

Bánh mì is one of the most popular street foods in Vietnam, and perhaps even the world. The name can refer to both the sandwich and the baguette itself. If you can't find the Vietnamese baguette (which is smaller and lighter than a French baguette, with a crispier crust), use a French baguette, halved crossways.

Traditionally eaten for breakfast, bánh mì has evolved into an all-day street food. The filling options are limitless, but usually include pâté and vegetables, plus coriander and a dressing. For the vegan version, you can use tofu, tempeh, mushrooms or vegan meat substitutes. Vegan pâté is available at many supermarkets.

BÁNH MÌ BAGUETTE SANDWICH

- 100 g (3½ oz) carrot, julienned
- 100 g (3½ oz) daikon (white radish), julienned
- ½ teaspoon salt
- 90 ml (3 fl oz) rice vinegar
- 3 tablespoons sugar
- 800 g (1 lb 12 oz) tender or semi-firm tofu, sliced
- 3 garlic cloves, finely chopped
- ½ teaspoon ground black pepper
- ½ teaspoon Chinese five-spice
- 90 ml (3 fl oz) soy sauce
- 1 tablespoon vegan oyster sauce
- 3 tablespoons canola (rapeseed) oil
- 2 bánh mì baguettes
- 60 g (2 oz) vegan pâté
- ½ red onion, thinly sliced
- 100 g (3½ oz) cucumber, thinly sliced
- 1 red chilli, destemmed and sliced
- 60 g (2 oz) vegan mayonnaise
- 2 coriander (cilantro) sprigs, chopped

In a bowl or jar, combine carrot, daikon and salt, and set aside to rest for 15 minutes. Drain any excess water from the vegetables. Add vinegar, sugar and 200 ml (7 fl oz) of water, cover and set aside to pickle for 2 hours. Drain the liquid.

Combine the tofu, garlic, black pepper, five-spice, soy sauce and vegan oyster sauce in a small dish and set aside to marinate for 30 minutes.

Heat a non-stick pan over medium–high heat and, once hot, add oil and the marinated tofu. Pan-fry until both sides of the tofu are slightly brown, then remove from pan.

Split the baguettes open down one side without completely splitting them in two. Spread the inside base of each baguette with the vegan pâté, then add the tofu, pickled carrot and daikon, red onion, cucumber, chilli, vegan mayonnaise and coriander. Close each baguette and serve.

PREPARATION TIME
15 minutes

COOKING TIME
15 minutes

MAKES
2 × 26 cm (10¼ in) pancakes

Also known as the Vietnamese crepe, 'bánh xèo' means 'sizzling cake', which refers to the sound of the batter being poured onto the hot iron pan. It is a thin, crispy rice flour pancake, traditionally stuffed with shrimp, pork and fresh herbs or greens. Vegan mince works just as well in place of meat, while the addition of turmeric gives the pancake a vivid golden colour.

Bánh xèo is very popular across Vietnam. The two main variations are from Miền Trung in central Vietnam and Miền Tây from the Mekong Delta region. The Miền Trung style is smaller and contains fewer fillings, while this version (Miền Tây) is larger, with more fillings, and the pancake is thinner and crispier.

BÁNH XÈO
CRISPY RICE PANCAKE

- 60 g (2 oz) rice flour
- 20 g (¾ oz) plain (all-purpose) wheat flour
- 2 teaspoons ground turmeric
- ½ teaspoon salt
- 150 ml (5 fl oz) coconut cream
- 90 ml (3 fl oz) canola (rapeseed) oil
- 60 g (2 oz) onion, thinly sliced
- 1 garlic clove, finely chopped
- 100 g (3½ oz) vegan mince
- 100 g (3½ oz) bean sprouts
- 2 spring onions (scallions), sliced
- 2 tablespoons crisp fried shallots or fried onion
- 4 lettuce leaves
- 4 mint sprigs
- 2 Thai basil sprigs
- 50 ml (1¾ fl oz) Nước chấm (page 20)

In a bowl, mix the flours, turmeric, half of the salt, the coconut cream and 180 ml (6 fl oz/¾ cup) of water. Strain through a sieve to remove any lumps and obtain a smooth batter.

Heat a non-stick frying pan over medium heat and, once hot, add 2 tablespoons of the oil and the onion, garlic and vegan mince, using a spatula to break up the mince. Cook for 2–3 minutes until the colour changes and the ingredients are all cooked. Add remaining salt and mix to combine. Transfer the mixture to a bowl.

Clean the pan and heat it up again over medium–high heat. Once hot, add 2 tablespoons of the oil and pour in a thin layer of the batter. Once the batter starts to set, add half of the filling and half of the bean sprouts on top of one-half of the pancake, then cover the pan and cook for another 2–3 minutes, until the batter is completely cooked. Uncover and cook for another 1–2 minutes, until the base of the pancake is crispy (be careful that it doesn't burn). Fold the pancake in half over the filling and transfer to a serving dish. Repeat with the remaining batter, filling and bean sprouts to make the second pancake.

Sprinkle the pancakes with spring onion and fried shallots and serve with the lettuce, mint, Thai basil and nước chấm.

PREPARATION TIME
5 minutes

MAKES
2 × 300 ml (10 fl oz) glasses

It is believed that coffee was first introduced to Vietnam by a French Catholic priest in 1857. By 1888, the country had its first coffee plantations and, today, it is the world's second-largest coffee producer. Coffee is deeply ingrained in daily life.

Vietnamese iced coffee is a rich, creamy, energising drink. You'll find different variations, but this is one of the most popular. It is made by brewing strong, dark local coffee using a traditional phin filter, then mixing it with sweetened condensed milk and ice. If you don't have a phin filter, you can use a normal coffee filter.

CÀ PHÊ SỮA ĐÁ
ICED COFFEE WITH CONDENSED MILK

- 60 g (2 oz) Vietnamese ground coffee (roasted between medium and dark, preferably Robusta coffee)
- 60 ml (2 fl oz/¼ cup) Coconut condensed milk (page 28)
- 400 g (14 oz) ice cubes

If you have a phin filter, you will need to make one portion of coffee at a time. Add 30 g (1 oz) of the coffee to the filter, making sure the bottom of the filter is covered with coffee powder up to the edge, otherwise the water could run past the coffee too quickly while brewing.

Put the coffee strainer on the coffee powder, add 30 ml (1 fl oz) of hot water, wait for 20 seconds, then press the strainer more tightly on the coffee. Pour in 70 ml (2¼ fl oz) more hot water and let it drip until it's finished (generally around 8 minutes). Repeat to make the second portion.

If you are using a normal coffee filter, you can make both cups at once instead of repeating the process.

Divide the condensed milk, ice cubes and brewed coffee between two glasses and mix well before drinking.

PREPARATION TIME
6 hours 30 minutes

COOKING TIME
30 minutes

MAKES
4 × 350 ml (12 fl oz) glasses or cups

Chè ba màu is a traditional, nostalgic dessert with eye-catching colours made up of three distinct layers. It's usually served in clear cups so you can see the colourful layers.

The bottom layer is typically made of sweetened red (adzuki) beans, followed by a middle layer of mung beans and white beans, then a topping of green jelly, shaved ice and sweetened coconut cream. Since preparing three kinds of beans is time-consuming, I just use mung beans for the middle layer (peeled mung beans cook faster than other beans).

CHÈ BA MÀU
THREE-COLOURED DESSERT

- 100 g (3½ oz) peeled, dried mung beans
- 4 pandan leaves, roughly chopped
- 2 teaspoons agar-agar
- 75 g (2¾ oz/⅓ cup) sugar
- 6 pineapple leaves (optional)
- 500 ml (17 fl oz/ 2 cups) coconut cream
- 1 tablespoon cornflour (cornstarch)
- 200 g (7 oz) sweetened red (adzuki) beans
- 200 g (7 oz) shaved ice

Soak the peeled mung beans for at least 6 hours, but preferably overnight.

In a blender or food processor, blend the pandan leaves and 400 ml (13½ fl oz) of water until it becomes pandan juice. Strain the juice and discard any solids.

Put the strained juice in a saucepan over low heat, add the agar-agar and 1 tablespoon of the sugar and mix until everything is dissolved. Bring the mixture to the boil and continue stirring for 1–2 minutes, then pour the mixture into a mould or container that's at least 2 cm (¾ in) deep, and set aside to cool. Refrigerate for 30 minutes or until set, then slice the jelly into strips about 3 cm (1¼ in) long and 8 mm (⅓ in) wide.

Put the mung beans in a large saucepan and pour in enough water to cover them. Bring to the boil over high heat, then reduce heat to low, cover and cook for 15–20 minutes until the beans are tender. Drain the water, add 2 tablespoons of the sugar and mash the beans with a spoon or potato masher until smooth.

Mix the pineapple leaves, if using, and the coconut cream in a saucepan over medium heat and bring to the boil. Add remaining sugar and the cornflour and mix well until everything is dissolved. Turn off the heat, discard the pineapple leaves, and set aside to cool.

To assemble, add a layer of red beans to the bottom of each of four serving glasses or cups. Top with a layer of mung beans, a layer of pandan jelly and a layer of shaved ice. Pour in the coconut cream mixture and serve.

MALAYSIA

Under the influences of Malay, Chinese and Indian cuisines, the street food scene in Malaysia is one of a kind. At street markets and stalls, you'll find everything from Chinese-style noodles like char kway teow (page 138), to dim sum such as siu mai (siew mai) and har gow, to curries, breads and classic Malay delicacies like nasi lemak (page 132) and satay. Don't pass by the teh tarik stand without trying the frothy milk tea (page 147).

The ingredients used in Malaysian street food reflect this diversity. Many of the dishes and condiments popular in Malaysia have counterparts in other Southeast Asian cuisines, such as Singaporean and Indonesian, and they are prepared a bit differently in each country. A good example is the differences between the typical laksas and sambals prepared in Malaysia versus what is common in Singapore and Indonesia. Sauces and spices from different cultures blend together to create the deep, complex flavours for which Malaysian dishes are known. The bold use of fresh and dried herbs and spices creates a collision of sweet, savoury, spicy, sour, tangy, aromatic flavours that make Malaysian street food exciting and satisfying.

The rising street food scene in both Malaysia and Singapore led to the emergence of hawker centres, such as the famous Gurney Drive Hawker Centre in Penang. These are typically open-air complexes with arrays of food stalls run by individual vendors, each with their own specialities. The centres provide a more organised and hygienic environment for dining, and make it easier for visitors to try many different kinds of street foods at once without running from place to place.

PREPARATION TIME
30 minutes

COOKING TIME
15 minutes

SERVES
2

Known as the national dish of Malaysia, nasi lemak is typically eaten for breakfast, but can also be enjoyed at other times of day. It is also quite popular in Singapore, Southern Thailand and some regions of Indonesia where there are ethnic Malay populations.

Nasi lemak is fragrant rice cooked with coconut milk and pandan leaves. In Malay, 'nasi' means 'rice' and 'lemak' means 'richness', in reference to the generous use of coconut milk. In Malaysia, the dish is traditionally served with fried anchovies, peanuts, cucumber and various other toppings. Meat such as ayam goreng berempah (Malay-spiced fried chicken) is often added, but for this vegan version, I use king oyster mushrooms.

NASI LEMAK (COCONUT RICE WITH TOPPINGS)

- 200 g (7 oz) jasmine rice
- 200 ml (7 fl oz) coconut cream
- 1 teaspoon salt
- 1 lemongrass stalk, smacked
- 2 pandan leaves
- 400 ml (13½ fl oz) canola (rapeseed) oil
- 300 g (10½ oz) fresh king oyster mushrooms, pulled into thin strips
- 1 batch (6 pieces) Malay-spiced fried king oyster mushrooms (page 135)
- 100 g (3½ oz) cucumber, sliced
- 2 tablespoons Sambal (page 24)
- 60 g (2 oz) fried redskin peanuts

In a saucepan, combine rice, coconut cream, one-quarter of a teaspoon of the salt and 120 ml (4 fl oz) of water, and mix well. Add the lemongrass and pandan leaves and bring to the boil over high heat. Once boiling, reduce heat to low, cover and cook for 15 minutes. Discard the lemongrass and pandan leaves. You can also use a rice cooker.

Meanwhile, heat the oil in a large saucepan over medium–high heat. To check whether the oil is hot enough for deep-frying, hold a wooden chopstick in the oil. If it is immediately surrounded by tiny bubbles, the oil is ready to use. Deep-fry the fresh oyster mushrooms for about 10 minutes until brown and slightly crispy. Season with remaining salt.

Divide the rice between two serving plates. (If you would like to make rice domes, as shown in the photograph, place each serve of rice into a small, dome-shaped bowl, compressing it gently with the back of a spoon. Place a serving plate over the bowl. Flip the plate with the bowl pressed against it, tap the bottom of the bowl to loosen the rice, then gently lift the bowl, leaving the rice dome on the plate.) Serve with the Malay-spiced fried king oyster mushrooms, fried oyster mushrooms, cucumber, sambal and fried peanuts.

PREPARATION TIME
4 hours

COOKING TIME
10 minutes

MAKES
6

Spiced fried chicken (ayam goreng berempah) is a Malaysian dish known for its bold use of spices, enticing aroma and crispiness. It's usually made with marinated chicken thighs but, instead of chicken, I have used king oyster mushrooms. (Funnily enough, in Chinese, these are known as 'chicken thigh mushrooms'!) The crunchy outer layer, the juicy inside and the signature spicy punch all come together to make it irresistible.

'Ayam' goreng cendawan tiram can be eaten just like this, as a snack, but the best way to enjoy it is with rice and sambal, which makes it a perfect match for the coconut rice dish nasi lemak (page 132).

'AYAM' GORENG CENDAWAN TIRAM (MALAY-SPICED FRIED KING OYSTER MUSHROOMS)

- 30 g (1 oz) galangal, sliced
- 30 g (1 oz) fresh ginger, sliced
- 3 shallots, sliced
- 6 garlic cloves
- 8 dried chillies
- 2 lemongrass stalks, sliced
- 2 teaspoons salt
- 2 tablespoons curry powder
- 1 tablespoon ground turmeric
- 1 tablespoon ground coriander
- 1 tablespoon ground cumin
- 30 g (1 oz/¼ cup) cornflour (cornstarch)
- 6 king oyster mushrooms, halved lengthways
- 500 ml (17 fl oz/2 cups) canola (rapeseed) oil
- 10 curry leaves

Combine the galangal, ginger, shallot, garlic, dried chillies, lemongrass and 100 ml (3½ fl oz) of water in a food processor and mix on high speed to form a paste. Transfer the blended ingredients to a bowl and add salt, curry powder, turmeric, coriander, cumin and cornflour. Mix everything well then add the king oyster mushrooms and stir to coat in the paste. Set aside to marinate for at least 4 hours.

Heat the oil in a large saucepan over medium–high heat. To check whether the oil is hot enough for deep-frying, hold a wooden chopstick in the oil. If it is immediately surrounded by tiny bubbles, the oil is ready to use. Add the curry leaves and deep-fry until crisp. Remove from the oil using a slotted spoon.

Add the mushrooms and deep-fry for 3–5 minutes until golden, taking care not to burn the spices. Remove and place on a serving dish with the curry leaves to serve.

PREPARATION TIME
1 hour

COOKING TIME
45 minutes

SERVES
4

At food stalls across Penang, the air is filled with the enticing aroma of this speciality dish, also known as Penang laksa. 'Asam' refers to the tamarind that gives the laksa its signature sourness. The soup is traditionally made with mackerel (I use kelp and shiitake mushrooms) and rempah, a richly spiced, sauce-like paste. Every family has their own closely guarded rempah recipe! For the soybean paste, I buy the brand Healthy Boy.

ASAM LAKSA (TAMARIND-BASED RICE NOODLE SOUP)

- 1 kelp sheet about 10 cm x 15 cm (4 in x 6 in)
- 10 dried shiitake mushrooms
- 800 g (1 lb 12 oz) pineapple, peeled and sliced
- 90 ml (3 fl oz) Vegan fish sauce (page 18)
- 80 g (2¾ oz) tamarind paste
- 50 g (1¾ oz) coconut (palm) sugar
- salt, to taste
- 20 tofu puffs
- 1 kg (2 lb 3 oz) fresh round or flat rice noodles, or 500 g (1 lb 2 oz) dried round or thick rice noodles
- 1 shallot, sliced
- 6 birdseye chillies, destemmed and sliced
- 200 g (7 oz) cucumber, julienned
- 1 handful Vietnamese coriander (laksa leaves), sliced
- mint leaves, to serve

REMPAH

- 15 g (½ oz) dried chillies
- 80 g (2¾ oz) shallots
- 4 garlic cloves
- 5 fresh cayenne chillies
- 15 g (½ oz) fresh turmeric
- 20 g (¾ oz) galangal
- 1 lemongrass stalk
- 3 candlenuts
- 50 ml (1¾ fl oz) canola (rapeseed) oil
- 1 tablespoon soybean paste

To make the soup, combine the kelp, shiitake mushrooms and 1.5 litres (50 fl oz/6 cups) of water in a large saucepan and set aside to soak for 1 hour. Then, bring to the boil over medium heat and simmer for 15 minutes.

Meanwhile, to make the rempah, soak the dried chillies in water for 15 minutes, then drain. Slice the shallots, garlic, destemmed cayenne chillies, turmeric, galangal, lemongrass and candlenuts. Heat a non-stick frying pan over low–medium heat and, once hot, add the oil and all of the other rempah ingredients except the soybean paste. Stir for 2–3 minutes until aromatic, taking care not to burn. Transfer the mixture to a food processor, add the soybean paste and blend to form a smooth paste.

Heat a non-stick pan over low–medium heat and, once hot, add the rempah and stir-fry for 10–15 minutes until it darkens and thickens. Remove from heat.

Add the rempah and half the pineapple to the soup. Add vegan fish sauce, tamarind paste and coconut sugar, bring to the boil and cook for 10 minutes. Season to taste with salt, add the tofu puffs and cook for a further 5 minutes.

Cook the rice noodles according to packet instructions. Divide noodles between four serving bowls, then pour over the soup. Top each bowl with sliced shallot, birdseye chilli, remaining pineapple, cucumber, Vietnamese coriander and mint leaves.

PREPARATION TIME
15 minutes

COOKING TIME
10 minutes

SERVES
2

Once known as a 'poor man's meal', char kway teow has become one of Malaysia's most beloved street food dishes, especially in Penang. This flavour-packed stir-fry reflects Malaysia's rich multicultural heritage, having been introduced by Teochew immigrants from the Chaoshan region of Canton, China. 'Kway teow' is the pronunciation of '粿条' in Teochew Min (the Teochew dialect) and means rice noodles.

The flat rice noodles are tossed and fried with soy sauces over high heat, creating a smoky, slightly charred flavour known as 'wok hei' ('breath of the wok'). In this vegan version, I use tofu instead of meat and eggs.

CHAR KWAY TEOW (STIR-FRIED RICE NOODLES)

- 2 tablespoons soy sauce
- 1 tablespoon dark soy sauce
- 1 tablespoon vegan oyster sauce
- 2 tablespoons Vegan fish sauce (page 18)
- 1 teaspoon sugar
- 400 g (14 oz) fresh flat rice noodles, or 180 g (6½ oz) dried rice noodles (width 1 cm/½ in)
- 75 ml (2½ fl oz) canola (rapeseed) oil
- 300 g (10½ oz) tender or semi-firm tofu, sliced
- 2 garlic cloves, chopped
- 1½ tablespoons Sambal (page 24)
- 100 g (3½ oz) bean sprouts
- 60 g (2 oz) garlic chives

In a bowl, mix the soy sauces, vegan oyster sauce, vegan fish sauce and sugar. If you're using dried rice noodles, soak them in warm water for 15 minutes, then soak in hot water for 1 minute, then soak in cold water.

Heat a wok or non-stick frying pan over medium–high heat and, once hot, add 3 tablespoons of the oil. Pan-fry the tofu until both sides are slightly brown and crispy, then remove from the pan.

Increase heat to high and add remaining oil. Add the garlic and stir until aromatic. Add tofu and sambal, stir briefly, then add the rice noodles. Stir for 30 seconds to 1 minute, until the noodles are slightly charred on the outside, then add the soy sauce mixture.

Mix everything and keep tossing and stirring for 1–2 minutes, taking care not to break the noodles. When most of the sauce has evaporated, add bean sprouts, stir for 30 seconds, add garlic chives, stir for another 30 seconds, then serve.

PREPARATION TIME
3 hours

COOKING TIME
10 minutes

MAKES
4

Roti canai or roti prata is a flatbread introduced by the Mamak people. What sets it apart from Indian roti is the extra flaky and layered texture, which comes from stretching and folding the dough, and the generous use of ghee (substituted with vegan butter and oil here).

Also popular in Singapore, Indonesia, Thailand and China (where it is known as the 'Indian flying pancake'), roti canai is typically served with dal and other curries, and enjoyed with a cup of teh tarik (pulled milk tea). It also makes a satisfying dish on its own, or it can be eaten as a dessert, served with sugar and condensed milk.

ROTI CANAI (INDIAN-MALAYSIAN FLATBREAD)

- 1 teaspoon sugar
- ⅔ teaspoon salt
- 40 ml (1¼ fl oz) Coconut condensed milk (page 28)
- 300 g (10½ oz) plain (all-purpose) wheat flour
- 30 ml (1 fl oz) corn (maize) oil, plus extra for greasing
- 30 g (1 oz) vegan butter, melted

In a large bowl, mix sugar, salt, condensed milk and 130 ml (4½ fl oz) of water until combined. Add the flour and knead it to form a dough. Place dough in a bowl, cover and let it rest for 30 minutes.

Knead the dough for 1–2 minutes (wear kitchen gloves to prevent it from sticking to your hands) and separate into 4 portions. Shape each portion into a round. Brush extra oil over the surface of the dough rounds and place them, in a single layer, into a large container. Cover and set aside to rest for at least 2 hours.

Wearing kitchen gloves again, transfer rounds to an oiled kitchen counter. Using your palm, press each round flat and stretch it out as large as possible without breaking it. (Alternatively, use a rolling pin to roll the dough flat, before stretching it further.) Carefully lift each side of the thin sheet of dough and fold it into a square (each side about 15 cm/6 in long). Repeat with remaining rounds.

Heat a non-stick pan over medium heat. Add half of the oil and half of the vegan butter. Once hot, carefully place a piece of the roti canai into the pan. Pan-fry until both sides are golden and crisp. Repeat with remaining roti canai, adding extra oil and butter as needed.

PREPARATION TIME
15 minutes

COOKING TIME
20 minutes

SERVES
2

Translated as 'stuffed tofu', tauhu sumbat looks like a tiny sandwich made of fried tofu, stuffed with fresh vegetables like carrot, cucumber and bean sprouts. The filling is crunchy and refreshing, while the fried tofu is very crispy on the outside and tender on the inside.

Tauhu sumbat is often sold at food stalls and markets where other fried foods are sold, such as stuffed eggplants (aubergines) and chilli peppers. It is prepared fresh to order and normally served with a spicy dipping sauce or a sweet peanut sauce. A simple and tasty snack, it can be enjoyed on its own or paired with other dishes.

TAUHU SUMBAT (STUFFED FRIED TOFU)

600 ml (20½ fl oz) canola (rapeseed) oil

800 g (1 lb 12 oz) tender or semi-firm tofu, cut into triangular slices about 2 cm (¾ in) thick, each side about 4 cm (1½ in) to 5 cm (2 in) long

100 g (3½ oz) carrots, julienned

100 g (3½ oz) cucumber, julienned

50 g (1¾ oz) bean sprouts

DIPPING SAUCE

20 g (¾ oz) dried chillies

2 garlic cloves, chopped

50 g (1¾ oz) coconut (palm) sugar

1 teaspoon salt

1 teaspoon cornflour (cornstarch)

60 ml (2 fl oz/¼ cup) rice vinegar or coconut vinegar

To make the dipping sauce, soak the dried chillies in hot water for 15 minutes, then drain. Put the drained chilli, garlic and 150 ml (5 fl oz) of water in a small food processor and blend until smooth. Transfer the mixture to a saucepan over low–medium heat, add coconut sugar, salt and cornflour and mix well. Bring to the boil and cook for 1–2 minutes until the sauce thickens. Turn off the heat and add the vinegar.

Heat the oil in a large saucepan over medium–high heat. To check whether the oil is hot enough for deep-frying, hold a wooden chopstick in the oil. If it is immediately surrounded by tiny bubbles, the oil is ready to use.

Deep-fry the tofu until it is golden and crispy on the outside, then remove and place on a serving dish. Cut the middle of the tofu open without cutting completely through, and stuff with carrot, cucumber and bean sprouts. Serve with the dipping sauce.

PREPARATION TIME
15 minutes

COOKING TIME
15 minutes

SERVES
2

Cendol is a shaved ice dessert that originated in Indonesia. Colourful and very refreshing, its main ingredient is a green, worm-like pandan jelly. You can either make this jelly from scratch, as per the recipe below, or from a premixed cendol powder (available from Asian stores). Lye water is a food-grade alkaline solution (also available from Asian stores) that adds a pleasant chewiness to the cendol.

Preparation varies by region. In Malaysia, cendol is made with mung bean starch and topped with shaved ice, red beans, sweet corn, coconut (palm) sugar, and sometimes fresh durian, though you can use any fruits you like.

CENDOL (SWEET ICED DESSERT WITH GREEN JELLY)

CENDOL

- 6 pandan leaves, roughly chopped
- 20 g (¾ oz) mung bean (green bean) starch
- 15 g (½ oz) tapioca flour
- 1 teaspoon lye (alkaline) water
- 300 g (10½ oz) ice cubes

TOPPINGS

- 80 g (2¾ oz) coconut (palm) sugar
- 400 ml (13½ fl oz) coconut milk
- 1 pandan leaf
- ½ teaspoon salt
- 600 g (1 lb 5 oz) shaved ice
- 65 g (2¼ oz/⅓ cup) sweet corn
- 200 g (7 oz) sweetened red (adzuki) beans

To make the cendol, put pandan leaf and 220 ml (7½ fl oz) of water in a blender and blitz until it has become pandan juice. Strain and discard solids. In a large bowl, mix the mung bean starch, tapioca flour, lye water and strained pandan juice.

Pour the mixture into a saucepan over low heat. Cook, stirring constantly, for a few minutes until the mixture thickens and has a texture similar to pudding. Remove from the heat.

Put the ice cubes in a large bowl and pour in enough water to cover them. While the cooked mixture is still warm, place some of it on a large slotted spoon or ladle, hold it over the iced water and press it through the holes with a big spoon or silicone spatula. The cooked batter will fall into the iced water, which helps to maintain its shape and elasticity.

To make the toppings, combine coconut sugar with 100 ml (3½ fl oz) of water in a small saucepan over low–medium heat for 2–3 minutes until the liquid becomes dense and syrup-like.

In another saucepan, combine the coconut milk, pandan leaf and salt. Bring to the boil over medium heat, then remove from heat and set aside to cool. Once cooled, discard the pandan leaf.

Divide the shaved ice between two serving bowls and pour over the cooled coconut mixture. Divide the cendol, sweet corn, sweetened red beans and syrup between the bowls and serve.

PREPARATION TIME
5 minutes

COOKING TIME
10 minutes

MAKES
2 × 450 ml (15 fl oz) glasses over ice or 2 × 300 ml (10 fl oz) glasses if served hot

Teh tarik is a sweet, creamy drink that's very popular in Malaysia's street food scene, where it is often enjoyed with dishes such as nasi lemak (page 132) and roti canai (page 140). Introduced by the Mamak people, the method of tea 'pulling' involves pouring the tea back and forth between two containers, from high up, to aerate it and make it taste richer and smoother.

Since most people do not have a cotton tea strainer like those used in Malaysia for pulled tea, I brew the tea first, then discard the powder and pull the tea. While it's often served hot, I find this iced version very refreshing. You can drink it from anything – big glasses, mugs, pots or jars!

TEH TARIK (PULLED MILK TEA)

- 20 g (¾ oz) ceylon black tea powder
- 60 ml (2 fl oz/¼ cup) Coconut condensed milk (page 28)
- 120 ml (4 fl oz) plant-based milk
- sugar, to taste
- 300 g (10½ oz) ice cubes

Add the black tea powder to a tea bag/filter. Place 500 ml (17 fl oz/2 cups) of water in a small saucepan and bring to the boil. Reduce the heat to low, add the tea bag and brew over low heat for 8 minutes. Remove the tea bag.

To pull the tea, pour it from the saucepan into another pot in a thin, steady stream, creating some distance between the two vessels (the saucepan should be at least 50 centimetres or 20 inches higher than the pot – the higher the better). Then, switch the vessels, holding the pot above, and pour the tea back into the saucepan. Repeat this process four times.

Add condensed milk, plant-based milk and sugar to taste, and stir well. Pull the tea again back and forth six times. It should become frothy.

Divide the ice cubes between two glasses and pour over the tea.

SINGAPORE

Singapore became independent from Malaysia in 1965 and the food culture of the two states remains deeply intertwined. Singaporean cuisine is also influenced by Chinese, Indian and Peranakan cuisines. Many dishes and street snacks are shared with other Southeast Asian regions, albeit with variations in preparation and ingredients. For example, the beloved laksa, which can be found in Singapore, Malaysia and Indonesia, varies not only between countries but also between regions within countries, with each region putting its own spin on the spicy noodle soup.

The nuances of each cuisine's take on classic dishes is only obvious when you fully immerse yourself in the street food scene.

Since its independence, Singapore's food has become more international and diverse, but some dishes remain exclusively Singaporean: for example, the iconic Hainanese chicken rice and the beloved breakfast dish of kaya toast (page 156). The hawker centre at Lau Pa Sat is a great place to try local and other Southeast Asian street foods in Singapore.

PREPARATION TIME
15 minutes

COOKING TIME
30 minutes

SERVES
4

Katong laksa is a beloved Singaporean dish created by the Peranakans of Katong. It features thick rice noodles cut short, so it can be eaten easily with a spoon – no chopsticks or fork required!

The rich, fragrant broth is usually made from rempah, prawn stock and coconut milk. Common toppings include prawns, cockles and fish cake, but here I've used tofu puffs and hearty king oyster mushrooms. It's traditionally garnished with laksa leaves (often called Vietnamese coriander or Vietnamese mint), which give the dish its distinctive aroma. If you can't find them, you can use standard coriander instead.

KATONG LAKSA (COCONUT CURRY NOODLES)

- 4 king oyster mushrooms
- 800 ml (27 fl oz) vegetable stock
- 800 ml (27 fl oz) coconut cream
- salt, to taste
- 20 tofu puffs
- 1 kg (2 lb 3 oz) fresh round or thick rice noodles, or 500 g (1 lb 2 oz) dried round or thick rice noodles
- 1 handful Vietnamese coriander (laksa leaves), sliced

REMPAH

- 50 ml (1¾ fl oz) canola (rapeseed) oil
- 15 g (½ oz) dried chillies, soaked in water for 15 minutes, then drained
- 4 garlic cloves
- 80g (2¾ oz) shallots, sliced
- 5 fresh cayenne chillies, destemmed and sliced
- 3 candlenuts
- 15 g (½ oz) fresh turmeric, sliced
- 20 g (¾ oz) galangal, sliced
- 1 lemongrass stalk, sliced
- 1 tablespoon soybean paste

Slice the mushrooms horizontally into pieces about 2 cm (¾ in) thick (separating the stems from the caps), then make some decorative cuts on each slice.

To make the rempah, heat a non-stick frying pan over low–medium heat and, once hot, add all the rempah ingredients except the soybean paste. Stir for 2–3 minutes until aromatic, taking care not to burn the ingredients.

Transfer the mixture to a food processor, add soybean paste and blend to form a smooth paste.

Heat a non-stick frying pan over medium heat and, once hot, add the rempah and stir-fry for about 10–15 minutes until the rempah darkens and thickens.

Put vegetable stock in a large saucepan over high heat and bring to the boil. Add the rempah and coconut cream, mix everything and add salt to taste. Add the tofu puffs and king oyster mushrooms, then reduce heat to low–medium and simmer for 10 minutes.

Cook the rice noodles according to packet instructions, then drain. Using kitchen scissors, cut the noodles into shorter pieces and divide between four serving bowls. Divide broth and toppings between bowls and garnish with Vietnamese coriander.

PREPARATION TIME
15 minutes

COOKING TIME
10 minutes

SERVES
2

Created under the influences of Malay, Javanese and Teochew culinary traditions, satay bee hoon is a fusion dish that reflects Singapore's rich multicultural heritage. With a base of rice vermicelli noodles (bee hoon), it is typically topped with seafood (I use tofu puffs instead), vegetables and a generous amount of satay sauce.

Saus saté (satay sauce) is essential to Singaporean street food – every street vendor and restaurant has their own recipe. The rich, nutty sauce is at the heart of this dish – it adds so much flavour and creaminess to the other ingredients.

SATAY BEE HOON (RICE VERMICELLI WITH SATAY SAUCE)

- 2 king oyster mushrooms
- 3 tablespoons canola (rapeseed) oil
- 200 g (7 oz) Saus saté (page 27)
- 2 tablespoons kecap manis (sweet soy sauce)
- 200 g (7 oz) dried rice vermicelli
- 200 g (7 oz) water spinach, cut into 4 cm (1½ in) lengths
- 20 tofu puffs, sliced
- 1 green chilli, destemmed and sliced

Slice the mushrooms about 2 cm (¾ in) thick, then make some decorative cuts on the mushroom slices.

Heat a non-stick frying pan over high heat and, once hot, add the oil and king oyster mushrooms and pan-fry until both sides are golden.

Combine the saus saté, kecap manis and 90 ml (3 fl oz) of water in a saucepan over medium heat and bring to the boil. Remove from heat.

Soak the rice vermicelli in hot water for 5 minutes, then drain.

Bring a saucepan of water to the boil, add water spinach, cook for 1 minute, then remove from water. Add rice vermicelli and cook for 1 minute, then drain and transfer vermicelli to a plate.

Pour the saté/kecap manis sauce over the vermicelli, then add the tofu puffs, water spinach and king oyster mushrooms. Sprinkle with green chilli and mix before serving.

PREPARATION TIME
15 minutes

COOKING TIME
10 minutes

SERVES
2

This classic dish, consisting of rice noodles and yellow noodles stir-fried in a rich broth, is generally served with calamansi lime and sambal. If you can't find calamansi lime, use regular lime.

Singaporean hokkien mee is very different from its Malaysian counterpart, which consists of thick yellow noodles fried in dark soy sauce. The Singaporean version was invented by an ex-sailor from Fujian (Hokkien) in the 1930s. It was originally known as rochor mee because the sailor sold the dish at his stall on Rochor Road. These days, you'll find hokkien mee at hawker centres all over Singapore.

HOKKIEN MEE (STIR-FRIED VERMICELLI)

- 80 g (2¾ oz) rice vermicelli
- 200 g (7 oz) fresh hokkien (yellow) noodles
- 90 ml (3 fl oz) canola (rapeseed) oil
- 400 g (14 oz) tender or semi-firm tofu, sliced
- 3 garlic cloves, chopped
- 60 ml (2 fl oz/¼ cup) Vegan fish sauce (page 18)
- 500 ml (17 fl oz/2 cups) vegetable stock
- 100 g (3½ oz) bean sprouts
- 100 g (3½ oz) garlic chives
- salt, to taste
- 2 tablespoons Sambal (page 24)
- ½ lime

Soak the rice vermicelli in lukewarm water for 15 minutes, then drain.

Cook the hokkien noodles for 2 minutes less than the packet instructions, then drain.

Heat a wok or non-stick frying pan over medium–high heat and, once hot, add 3 tablespoons of the oil and the tofu. Pan-fry the tofu until both sides are slightly brown and crisp. Remove from pan.

Increase the heat to high, add the remaining oil and the garlic to the wok or pan and stir until aromatic. Add the hokkien noodles, rice vermicelli and vegan fish sauce and cook, stirring, for 1 minute. Add half of the vegetable stock, mix a little, then cover and cook for 2 minutes.

Uncover, add tofu and mix everything a little. Add the remaining stock and keep tossing and stirring, being careful not to break the noodles. When half of the sauce has been absorbed, add bean sprouts, stir for 30 seconds, then add garlic chives. Stir for another 30 seconds, then season to taste with salt. Serve with sambal and lime on the side.

PREPARATION TIME
5 minutes

COOKING TIME
35 minutes

MAKES
4

Invented by Hainanese immigrants who came to Singapore in the early twentieth century, kaya toast is a traditional breakfast that's also enjoyed as a snack, normally with a cup of kopi (strong local coffee) or teh (tea). It's typically found at kopitiams (coffee shops), local eateries and food stalls.

Despite its simplicity, kaya toast – which is like a sweet sandwich – has become a symbol of Singaporean food culture and is much-loved by locals. Eggs are usually used to thicken the jam, but for a vegan version, cornflour (cornstarch) works well. Salted caramel sauce is available at many supermarkets (or you can make your own).

KAYA TOAST (TOAST WITH COCONUT JAM)

- 8 slices white bread
- 30 g (1 oz) vegan butter, sliced

KAYA JAM

- 300 ml (10 fl oz) coconut milk
- 2 pandan leaves, cut into 3 cm (1¼ in) pieces
- 100 g (3½ oz) coconut (palm) sugar
- 2 tablespoons salted caramel sauce
- ¼ teaspoon salt
- 1 tablespoon cornflour (cornstarch)

To make the kaya jam, put coconut milk and pandan leaves in a saucepan over medium heat and bring to the boil. Remove from heat and set aside for 15 minutes.

Add coconut sugar, salted caramel sauce and salt to the pan, and mix until dissolved.

In a separate small bowl, mix the cornflour with 2 tablespoons of water, then pour into the pan. Return to the lowest heat and cook for 15–20 minutes until the jam thickens (keep stirring so it doesn't burn).

Take the pandan leaves out and wait for the jam to cool down. You can store the unused jam in an airtight container in the fridge for up to a week.

Toast the bread and spread each slice with the kaya jam. Add sliced butter to one piece of toast and sandwich with another piece of toast. Repeat with remaining bread.

Cut each kaya toast into pieces to serve.

INDONESIA

Indonesia is a multicultural country with more than 1300 recognised ethnic groups. The street food scene naturally reflects this diverse heritage, blending indigenous flavours with influences from various cultures, including Chinese, Malay, Indian and Arab cuisines.

The connection between Indonesian and Malaysian street food is obvious, as these countries share many cultural and historical ties, and their culinary traditions reflect the influence of traders and migrants who travelled between them. Many dishes, such as saté/satay (grilled meat skewers), rujak/rojak (mixed fruit and vegetable salad, page 170) and dadar gulung/kuih gulung (rolled coconut pandan pancakes, page 174) can be found in both cuisines, though they are named differently and their preparation and flavour profiles vary slightly.

What sets Indonesian street food apart from its Malaysian and Singaporean counterparts is the ubiquitous use of peanuts. Peanuts are commonly used to make sauces for dressing or dipping, adding richness and depth to the ingredients, and making them more enjoyable and satisfying. Peanut sauce is a staple accompaniment for dishes such as gado-gado (mixed salad, page 166), ketoprak (tofu and rice vermicelli salad, page 169), rujak buah (spicy fruit salad, page 170) and the famous saus saté (satay sauce, page 27).

PREPARATION TIME
15 minutes

COOKING TIME
10 minutes

SERVES
2

'Nasi' means rice in both Indonesian and Malay. As nasi lemak is the national dish of Malaysia, nasi goreng is, without doubt, the national dish of Indonesia. Wherever there are street food markets in Indonesia, there will be someone stir-frying rice in a hot wok to make this dish.

For this vegan version, I have used tempeh. The secrets to the dish are kecap manis (Indonesian sweet soy sauce), which gives a smoky, umami, slightly sweet flavour, and sambal, which adds savouriness and spiciness.

It's best to use 'overnight' rice (cooked the night before, then cooled and refrigerated), as it can better soak up the sauce and won't stick together.

NASI GORENG (FRIED RICE)

- 60 ml (2 fl oz/¼ cup) canola (rapeseed) oil
- 300 g (10½ oz) tempeh, diced
- 3 garlic cloves, chopped
- 2 red shallots, diced
- 2 fresh cayenne chillies, destemmed and diced
- 400 g (14 oz) overnight rice (preferably jasmine rice)
- 1 tablespoon Sambal (page 24)
- 3 tablespoons kecap manis (sweet soy sauce)
- 1 tablespoon soy sauce
- 1 tablespoon Vegan fish sauce (page 18)
- 1 spring onion (scallion), sliced
- 2 tablespoons crisp fried shallots or fried onion
- 60 g (2 oz) cucumber, thinly sliced

Heat a wok or frying pan over medium–high heat and, once hot, add 2 tablespoons of the oil and the tempeh, and pan-fry until slightly golden. Push the tempeh to the side, then add the remaining oil, garlic, shallot and cayenne chilli, and stir until aromatic.

Increase heat to high, add the rice and stir for 1 minute or so until the rice is well distributed in the wok. Add sambal, kecap manis, soy sauce and vegan fish sauce, stirring vigorously for 1–2 minutes until all the sauce is absorbed by the rice. Sprinkle with spring onion then divide the mixture between two serving plates.

Top each plate with fried shallots and serve with sliced cucumber.

PREPARATION TIME
15 minutes

COOKING TIME
10 minutes

SERVES
2

Very similar to mee goreng, which is popular in Malaysia and Singapore, this dish is a common street food in Indonesia. Street vendors toss the noodles over high heat, quickly stir-frying them with flavourful sauces and ingredients. The sizzling sounds, rich aroma and vibrant visuals make mie goreng an irresistible street food experience.

As with other fried noodles, there are no strict rules as to what you can and can't add, so use your preferred vegetables. Traditionally, chicken or prawns are used, but tempeh works very well for this vegan version. Instant noodles are ideal for stir-frying.

MIE GORENG (FRIED NOODLES)

- 2 tablespoons kecap manis (sweet soy sauce)
- 2 tablespoons dark soy sauce
- 2 tablespoons soy sauce
- 1½ tablespoons tomato sauce (ketchup)
- 1 tablespoon vegan oyster sauce
- 200 g (7 oz) dried noodles for frying (such as mie or instant noodles) or 300 g (10½ oz) fresh mie noodles
- 60 ml (2 fl oz/¼ cup) canola (rapeseed) oil
- 200 g (7 oz) tempeh, sliced
- 1 tablespoon sesame oil
- 2 garlic cloves, chopped
- 1 shallot, chopped
- 150 g (5½ oz) cabbage, sliced into thin strips
- 1 tablespoon Sambal (page 24)
- 120 g (4½ oz) bean sprouts
- 1 spring onion (scallion), sliced

Mix kecap manis, dark soy sauce, soy sauce, tomato sauce and vegan oyster sauce in a bowl.

If using instant noodles, soak in hot water until they are almost tender, then drain. (Do not soak for too long, otherwise they will get soggy.) If using fresh noodles, cook for 1 minute less than the cooking time specified on the packet instructions, then drain.

Heat a wok or frying pan over medium–high heat. Once hot, add the canola oil and tempeh and pan-fry until both sides are golden and slightly crispy. Remove from pan.

Add the sesame oil to the wok, then add garlic and shallot and cook, stirring, for 30 seconds. Increase heat to high, add the cabbage, stir for 1 minute, then add sambal, stir for 30 seconds then add the noodles.

Stir for 1 minute, then add the sauce mixture and mix everything well. Continue to cook, stirring, for 2–3 minutes until most of the sauce is absorbed. Add the bean sprouts, stir for 30 seconds, then add the spring onion and stir for another 30 seconds before serving.

PREPARATION TIME
3 hours

COOKING TIME
1 hour 15 minutes

MAKES
6 rolls

Lontong is a compressed rice cake, wrapped and cooked in banana leaves to give a distinct taste and aroma. A versatile staple, it can be used in dishes such as soups, stews and curries, and it makes a great substitute for ordinary rice. It is often served at street food stands alongside dishes such as gado-gado (page 166), the spicy vegetable stew lontong sayur, and ketoprak (page 169).

Lontong can be stored in the fridge for up to 3 days or frozen for up to 2 months. To reheat it before eating, cut it into chunks and steam it for 5 minutes (if refrigerated) or 15 minutes (if frozen).

LONTONG (RICE CAKES IN BANANA LEAVES)

- 300 g (10½ oz) jasmine rice
- ½ teaspoon salt
- 1 lemongrass stalk, smacked
- 3 pandan leaves
- 6 banana leaf pieces, each about 30 × 40 cm (12 in x 15¾ in)

Mix rice, salt and 360 ml (12 fl oz) of water in a saucepan over high heat. Add the lemongrass and pandan leaves and bring to the boil. Reduce to the lowest heat, cover and cook for about 15 minutes. (Alternatively, use a rice cooker.) Discard the lemongrass and pandan leaves.

Bring a saucepan filled with enough water to cover the banana leaf pieces to the boil. Add the banana leaf and simmer for 1 minute. Remove from the pan, drain and leave to cool slightly.

When the rice is cool enough to handle, take one-sixth of the rice and place it on a piece of banana leaf, about 5 cm (2 in) from the long edge. Using your fingers, form the rice into a rough cylinder shape on the leaf.

Tightly roll the long edge of the banana leaf around the rice filling. Both ends of the roll should be open at this point. Use kitchen string to tie both ends firmly. It is important that the ends are tied tightly so that the rice does not fall out and water does not get inside the roll when it is cooked.

Fill a large saucepan with water and bring to the boil. Reduce heat to low–medium and add the rice rolls, making sure they are fully submerged. Cover and simmer for 1 hour. Remove from the pan and set aside to cool.

Once cooled, refrigerate for 2 hours to allow the rice to firm up fully. Cut into pieces and serve with your favourite dishes.

PREPARATION TIME
30 minutes

COOKING TIME
20 minutes

SERVES
2

'Gado-gado', meaning 'mix-mix', is a plate of fresh, colourful ingredients mixed together and coated with rich, tangy peanut sauce. It generally includes several steamed or cooked vegetables, such as potatoes and green beans, and raw vegetables like tomatoes, cucumbers, lettuce, cabbage, carrots and bean sprouts. Plant-based protein, such as tempeh or tofu, are often added.

Despite being a salad, the dish is typically served with rice or lontong (page 164). For extra crispiness, you can top it with emping (vegan chips made from melinjo nuts).

GADO-GADO (MIXED SALAD WITH PEANUT SAUCE)

- 200 g (7 oz) tofu, sliced and pan-fried
- 150 g (5½ oz) tempeh, sliced and pan-fried
- 100 g (3½ oz) green beans, cooked and cut into 3 cm (1¼ in) lengths
- 200 g (7 oz) potatoes, peeled, cooked and diced
- 100 g (3½ oz) bean sprouts
- 100 g (3½ oz) lettuce, thinly sliced
- 100 g (3½ oz) tomatoes, cut into wedges
- 100 g (3½ oz) carrots, julienned
- 100 g (3½ oz) cucumber, sliced
- 2 tablespoons crisp fried shallots or fried onion
- 10 emping or other vegan chips (optional)
- 200 g (7 oz) Lontong (page 164), cut into pieces and reheated

PEANUT SAUCE

- 3 tablespoons canola (rapeseed) oil, plus extra for frying
- 200 g (7 oz) roasted and salted peanuts
- 5 garlic cloves
- 3 birdseye chillies, destemmed
- 2 tablespoons coconut (palm) sugar
- 2 tablespoons lime juice
- 1 tablespoon tamarind sauce
- salt, to taste

To make the peanut sauce, heat a saucepan over low–medium heat. Add the extra oil (for frying) and peanuts, and stir until the peanuts are slightly brown. Remove from the pan and transfer to a small food processor.

Add garlic, chilli, oil and 300 ml (10 fl oz) of water to the food processor and blend on high speed to form a smooth paste. Alternatively, you can pound peanuts, garlic and chilli using a mortar and pestle until they are finely crushed, then add the oil and 300 ml (10 fl oz) of water, and keep pounding until it turns into a paste.

Return the paste to the pan over low–medium heat. Add the coconut sugar, lime juice, tamarind sauce and salt to taste. Cook, stirring for a few minutes, until the paste darkens and thickens. Remove from heat.

Assemble all the salad ingredients except the fried shallots, emping and lontong on a serving plate. Pour over the peanut sauce and sprinkle with the shallots. Mix everything well, garnish with emping (if using) and serve with the lontong.

PREPARATION TIME
15 minutes

COOKING TIME
10 minutes

SERVES
2

Vendors pushing trolleys labelled 'KETOPRAK' in large letters are a common sight throughout Indonesian neighborhoods, and food stalls selling ketoprak can be found at many local markets. A traditional vegetarian salad dish from Jakarta, ketoprak can easily be made vegan. It's served with lontong (page 164) or ketupat (rice cakes), rice vermicelli, fried tofu, bean sprouts, peanut sauce, crisp fried shallots and krupuk (prawn crackers), which can be replaced with vegan chips such as emping.

KETOPRAK (TOFU AND RICE VERMICELLI SALAD)

- 50 g (1¾ oz) dried rice vermicelli
- 200 g (7 oz) Lontong (page 164), cut into pieces and reheated
- 10 tofu puffs, halved
- 50 g (1¾ oz) bean sprouts, boiled for 15 seconds
- 50 g (1¾ oz) cucumber, sliced
- 2 tablespoons crisp fried shallots or fried onion
- 10 emping or other vegan chips

PEANUT SAUCE

- 3 garlic cloves
- 3 birdseye chillies, destemmed
- 50 g (1¾ oz) roasted and salted peanuts, crushed
- 2 tablespoons coconut (palm) sugar
- 1 teaspoon salt
- 2 tablespoons kecap manis (sweet soy sauce)

To make the peanut sauce, use a mortar and pestle to pound the garlic and chilli until they are smacked. Add the peanuts and pound until the mixture becomes a paste, then add coconut sugar and salt. Pound for a further minute, then add the kecap manis and 75 ml (2½ fl oz) of water, and mix everything well.

Soak the rice vermicelli in hot water for 10 minutes, then drain.

Divide the vermicelli, lontong, tofu puffs, bean sprouts, cucumber and peanut sauce between two serving plates. Garnish with fried shallots and emping.

PREPARATION TIME
15 minutes

SERVES
2

A refreshing yet spicy fruit and vegetable salad, rujak is considered to be one of the oldest Javanese dishes. Also a popular street food in Malaysia (where it is called 'rojak') and Singapore, its preparation differs depending on the region and its tradition.

This is a recipe for rujak buah (fruit rujak). At food stalls, vendors will pound the chilli dressing and mix it with your choice of fruit (most commonly unripe mango, jicama, water apple, pineapple or cucumber). The condiment air asam jawa (tamarind water) is available in Asian stores, but if you can't get it, substitute with tamarind sauce.

RUJAK BUAH (SPICY FRUIT SALAD)

- 150 g (5½ oz) roasted and salted peanuts
- 80 g (2¾ oz) coconut (palm) sugar
- 5 birdseye chillies, destemmed
- 3 tablespoons air asam jawa (tamarind water) or tamarind sauce
- salt, to taste
- 300 g (10½ oz) mango (green or not too ripe), peeled and cut into chunks
- 200 g (7 oz) green apple, cored and cut into chunks
- 200 g (7 oz) papaya (green or not too ripe), peeled and cut into chunks
- 200 g (7 oz) pineapple (not too ripe), peeled and cut into chunks
- 150 g (5½ oz) cucumber, thickly sliced

Using a mortar and pestle, pound the peanuts, coconut sugar, chilli, air asam jawa or tamarind sauce and 60 ml (2 fl oz/¼ cup) of water until the mixture becomes a paste. Season with salt.

Combine the mango, apple, papaya, pineapple and cucumber in a large bowl. Add the paste and toss until well combined.

PREPARATION TIME
8 hours

COOKING TIME
20 minutes

SERVES
2

Saté (grilled meat skewers) can often be found cooking on charcoal grills on the streets of Indonesia. The most common saté are saté ayam (chicken saté) and saté kambing (lamb saté). Always paired with saus saté, which adds a rich, nutty flavour, they may also be served with lontong.

For this vegan version, I've replaced the meat with seitan (also known as vital wheat gluten). I've included instructions for cooking in a frying pan if you don't have a charcoal grill.

SATÉ SEITAN (SEITAN SKEWERS WITH SATÉ SAUCE)

- 1 teaspoon garlic powder
- 1 teaspoon onion powder
- 1 teaspoon ground coriander
- 1 teaspoon ground cumin
- ½ teaspoon ground turmeric
- 2 tablespoons kecap manis (sweet soy sauce)
- 1 tablespoon air asam jawa (tamarind water) or tamarind sauce
- 1 tablespoon coconut (palm) sugar
- 1 teaspoon salt
- 300 g (10½ oz) seitan (vital wheat gluten) flour
- 1 lemongrass stalk, sliced
- 6 garlic cloves
- 3 shallots, finely chopped
- 20 g (¾ oz) galangal, sliced
- 60 ml (2 fl oz/¼ cup) soy sauce
- 3 tablespoons canola (rapeseed) oil, plus extra 3 tablespoons (if pan-frying)
- 150 g (5½ oz) Saus saté (page 27)

In a bowl, mix garlic powder, onion powder, coriander, cumin, turmeric, kecap manis, air asam jawa or tamarind sauce, coconut sugar, salt and 350 ml (12 fl oz) of water. Add the seitan flour, mix everything together and knead it into a flat dough about 1 cm (½ in) thick. (The amount of liquid needed for the seitan flour depends on the brand. If there is still dry flour that you cannot knead into the dough after you've added the coconut milk and water, just add a bit more water.) Let the dough rest for 30 minutes, then cut it into chunks about 1 cm (½ in) wide.

Bring a large saucepan of water to the boil. Add seitan chunks and cook for 10 minutes. Drain.

Mix lemongrass, garlic, shallot, galangal, soy sauce and oil in a food processor and blend the mixture until it had turned into puree. Coat the seitan chunks evenly with the pureed mixture, and set aside to marinate for at least 6 hours, or preferably overnight, in the fridge.

Preheat a charcoal grill. Thread the seitan chunks onto barbecue skewers. Grill until they are slightly charred on the outside.

You can also cook these in a frying pan. Heat a non-stick pan over medium heat and, once hot, add the extra 3 tablespoons of oil. Place the skewers in the pan and fry on both sides until slightly charred and crispy. Serve with saus saté.

PREPARATION TIME
45 minutes

COOKING TIME
20 minutes

MAKES
8

Dadar gulung is a traditional Indonesian rolled pancake with a filling of grated coconut and coconut (palm) sugar. 'Dadar' means 'pancake' or 'omelette' and 'gulung' means 'to roll'. It is also popular in Malaysia, Brunei and Singapore.

Pandan leaves give the pancake a bright green colour and a distinct aroma. The batter is usually made with eggs, which I have omitted for the vegan version. The soft, chewy texture of the pancake and the rich sweetness of the filling make a very satisfying combination, and it is convenient to take away as a snack or dessert.

DADAR GULUNG (ROLLED COCONUT PANDAN PANCAKES)

- 400 ml (13½ fl oz) coconut milk
- 6 pandan leaves, roughly chopped
- 150 g (5½ oz) plain (all-purpose) wheat flour
- 2 tablespoons cornflour (cornstarch)
- 150 g (5½ oz) fresh coconut flesh, grated
- 150 g (5½ oz) coconut (palm) sugar
- ¾ teaspoon salt

Combine the coconut milk and 4 of the pandan leaves in a food processor and mix until very smooth. In a big bowl, mix the wheat flour, cornflour, coconut milk mixture and one-quarter of a teaspoon of the salt. Strain the batter through a sieve to make sure there are no lumps. Set aside to rest for 30 minutes.

Cut the remaining 2 pandan leaves into thin strips. Mix the grated coconut, coconut sugar, pandan leaf strips and remaining half-teaspoon of salt in a saucepan over low heat. Cook, stirring so that it does not burn, until the sugar is dissolved. Add 60 ml (2 fl oz/¼ cup) of water and keep stirring until all the liquid has been absorbed and the mixture is golden brown. Leave for a few minutes to cool slightly.

Heat a non-stick frying pan (preferably with a diameter of around 20 cm/8 in) over low heat. Ladle about one-third of a cup of batter into the pan and spread it evenly over the base. Cook for 2–3 minutes, until the pancake is set and has turned slightly darker green, then remove from the pan and set aside. Repeat with remaining batter to make 8 pancakes.

Place a few spoonfuls of the filling in each pancake and roll up as you would a burrito.

SOUTH KOREA

The history of street food in South Korea can be traced back to the fourteenth century, when food stalls started to emerge at local markets. Unique to the South Korean street food scene are stalls known as pojangmacha (or 'pocha'), which are characterised by their colourful awnings and casual outdoor seating.

Street food options were quite limited before the 1960s, especially after the Korean War. The most common foods sold at food stalls were steamed buns such as jinppang, filled with red-bean paste, and hoppang, filled with vegetables and meat. Despite the lack of variety, street food provided low-cost meals for people who could not afford more at the time.

During the 1970s, the classic Korean dishes we know today, such as tteokbokki (page 184) and gimbap (page 186), began to trend, marking a rise in living standards. South Korea's street food scene is ever-evolving and the variety of dishes continues to increase. Although you'll always find traditional dishes, fusion foods such as the Korean corn dog (page 183) have also become popular.

PREPARATION TIME
15 minutes

COOKING TIME
10 minutes

SERVES
2

Japchae is a traditional Korean salad made with sweet potato starch noodles and various vegetables. Beef and egg strips are normally added, but for the vegan version, I use smoked tofu (available at the supermarket).

Traditionally served at festivals, celebrations or as a side dish, japchae can also be found at food stalls and markets. It's often prepared in bulk and served cold. The translucent, elastic and slightly chewy noodles absorb the flavours of the vegetables and the sauce, making for a colourful and satisfying dish. As it's quite light, it can be enjoyed at any time of day.

잡채

JAPCHAE (STIR-FRIED GLASS NOODLES)

- 60 g (2 oz) spinach leaves
- 1 teaspoon salt
- 100 g (3½ oz) dried sweet potato noodles
- 60 ml (2 fl oz/¼ cup) soy sauce
- 2 tablespoons sesame oil
- 2 teaspoons sugar
- 60 ml (2 fl oz/¼ cup) canola (rapeseed) oil
- 150 g (5½ oz) smoked tofu, thinly sliced
- 6 shiitake mushrooms, thinly sliced
- 5 g (⅛ oz) dried black fungus (wood ear mushrooms), soaked for 15 minutes, then drained and sliced
- 60 g (2 oz) onion, thinly sliced
- 60 g (2 oz) leek (white part only), julienned
- 60 g (2 oz) carrots, julienned
- 4 garlic cloves, chopped
- 1 capsicum (bell pepper), thinly sliced
- ½ teaspoon ground white pepper
- 2 tablespoons toasted sesame seeds

Bring a large saucepan of water to the boil and blanch the spinach for 15 seconds. Reserving the water, drain the spinach and mix with half a teaspoon of the salt.

Add the sweet potato noodles to the reserved water in the pan and simmer for 2–3 minutes. Turn off the heat and leave noodles to soak in the hot water for 5 minutes. Drain the water, return noodles to the pan and mix with 1 tablespoon of the soy sauce, 1 tablespoon of the sesame oil and the sugar.

Heat a wok over medium–high heat and, once hot, add the canola oil and smoked tofu and pan-fry for a little until slightly brown on both sides. Push the smoked tofu aside, add shiitake mushroom and dried black fungus and cook, stirring, for 1 minute.

Add onion, leek and carrot and cook, stirring, for 2–3 minutes until the ingredients are cooked. Add garlic and capsicum and stir for another minute, then add the noodles, white pepper and remaining salt, soy sauce and sesame oil, and stir for 2–3 minutes. Sprinkle with sesame seeds, mix everything well and serve.

PREPARATION TIME
30 minutes

COOKING TIME
15 minutes

SERVES
2

This is the vegan version of the very popular Korean fried chicken (dakgangjeong). The crispy, bite-sized tofu is deep-fried then coated in a sweet and spicy sauce to create an addictive dish that has multiple layers of flavours and textures.

Dakgangjeong is usually fried twice to achieve an extra-crispy texture, making it very crunchy on the outside and juicy on the inside. At street stalls, batches are fried and then served in small cups or paper cones to make it easy to eat while exploring a busy market or strolling around the city.

비건 두부강정

SWEET CRISPY KOREAN FRIED TOFU

- 500 g (17⅔ oz) tofu, diced about 1.5 cm (½ in) wide
- ½ teaspoon salt
- ½ teaspoon ground black pepper
- 200 ml (7 fl oz) plant-based milk
- 1 tablespoon garlic powder
- 5 garlic cloves, minced
- 3 tablespoons tomato sauce (ketchup)
- 1½ tablespoons sugar
- 1 tablespoon gochujang (Korean chilli paste)
- 2 tablespoons soy sauce
- 1 tablespoon chilli flakes
- 150 g (5½ oz) cornflour (cornstarch) or wheat starch
- 1 teaspoon baking powder
- 500 ml (17 fl oz/2 cups) canola (rapeseed) oil
- 1 tablespoon toasted sesame seeds

Marinate the tofu with salt, black pepper and milk for 30 minutes.

Meanwhile, in a bowl, mix the garlic powder and minced garlic, tomato sauce, sugar, gochujang, soy sauce, chilli flakes and 75 ml (2½ fl oz) of water.

In a separate bowl, mix the cornflour or wheat starch and baking powder.

Remove the tofu from the marinade and coat the pieces well with the flour mixture.

Heat the oil in a large saucepan over a medium–high heat. To check whether the oil is hot enough for deep-frying, hold a wooden chopstick in the oil. If it is immediately surrounded by tiny bubbles, the oil is ready to use.

Deep-fry the tofu for 3–5 minutes, until it is golden on the outside. Remove from the oil using a slotted spoon and drain on paper towel. To obtain extra crispiness, wait for 1 minute, then fry the tofu again for 1 minute.

Heat the sauce in a saucepan over medium heat. When it begins to bubble, add the tofu and quickly mix until it is evenly coated. Top with sesame seeds to serve.

PREPARATION TIME
1 hour 15 minutes

COOKING TIME
10 minutes

MAKES
4

The popularity of this trendy South Korean snack has spread worldwide. A twist on the classic American corn dog, the Korean corn dog is far more versatile and creative!

Usually coated with panko (Japanese) breadcrumbs, alternative coatings for Korean corn dogs are ramen noodles, diced cooked potatoes or even French fries. Alongside the frankfurt, cheese is also often added, and for this recipe, I use vegan versions of both. The contrast between the crispy exterior, the chewy middle and the melted cheese makes Korean corn dogs a distinctive and satisfying snack.

한국식 핫도그

KOREAN CORN DOGS (HANGUKSIK HAT DOGEU)

- 150 g (5½ oz) plain (all-purpose) wheat flour
- 1 teaspoon instant dried yeast
- 1 tablespoon sugar
- ½ teaspoon salt
- 150 ml (5 fl oz) plant-based milk
- 4 vegan frankfurts (sausages)
- 8 vegan cheese pieces about 2 cm x 3 cm (¾ in x 1¼ in)
- 100 g (3½ oz) panko (Japanese) breadcrumbs
- 600 ml (20½ fl oz) canola (rapeseed) oil
- 60 g (2 oz) vegan mayonnaise
- 60 g (2 oz) tomato sauce (ketchup)
- 30 g (1 oz) mustard

In a large bowl, mix the wheat flour with yeast, sugar, salt and plant-based milk. Mix with a chopstick until all the ingredients are well combined, then put a damp tea towel (dish towel) over the bowl and set aside to rest for 1 hour.

Push a vegan frankfurt and 2 vegan cheese pieces onto a barbecue skewer, then coat evenly with the batter, ensuring everything is well coated so the cheese won't leak while frying. Coat evenly with panko breadcrumbs. Repeat to make 4 skewers.

Heat the oil in a large saucepan over medium–high heat. To check whether the oil is hot enough for deep-frying, hold a wooden chopstick in the oil. If it is immediately surrounded by tiny bubbles, the oil is ready to use.

Deep-fry the corn dogs in batches until golden, then remove and place on a serving dish. Drizzle with vegan mayonnaise, tomato sauce and mustard to serve.

PREPARATION TIME
10 minutes

COOKING TIME
15 minutes

SERVES
2

These spicy rice cakes are perhaps Korea's most famous street food. 'Tteok' refers to the rice cakes and 'bokki' means 'stir-fried' or 'braised'. The tender, sticky texture of the rice cakes and the heat from the gochujang-based sauce makes an enticing combination.

Tteokbokki is typically served straight from the pot, and the warmth and spiciness of the dish make it incredibly comforting, especially on colder days. Garae-tteok, the rice cakes used to make tteokbokki, can be found in the refrigerated section in Asian stores.

떡볶이

TTEOKBOKKI (SPICY RICE CAKES)

- 300 g (10½ oz) garae-tteok
- 3 tablespoons gochujang (Korean chilli paste)
- 1 tablespoon gochugaru (Korean chilli flakes)
- 1 tablespoon tomato sauce (ketchup)
- 2 tablespoons sugar
- 1 teaspoon cornflour (cornstarch)
- 2 tablespoons soy sauce
- 3 tablespoons canola (rapeseed) oil
- 3 garlic cloves, chopped
- 50 g (1¾ oz) onion, sliced
- 60 g (2 oz) leek (white part only), sliced
- 100 g (3½ oz) cabbage, sliced
- 1 spring onion (scallion), sliced
- 1 tablespoon toasted white sesame seeds

Boil the garae-tteok according to packet instructions (normally 3–5 minutes), then soak in cold water. Drain.

In a bowl, mix the gochujang, gochugaru, tomato sauce, sugar, cornflour and soy sauce.

Heat a wok or non-stick frying pan over medium–high heat and, once hot, add oil, garlic, onion and leek. Stir for 1 minute, until aromatic, then add the cabbage and stir for another minute. Add the gochujang sauce mixture, stir a little, then add the garae-tteok and pour in 200 ml (7 fl oz) of hot water. Cover and let it simmer for a few minutes until the sauce thickens.

To serve the tteokbokki, sprinkle with spring onion and white sesame seeds.

PREPARATION TIME
15 minutes

COOKING TIME
15 minutes

SERVES
2 (makes 4 rolls)

Gimbap, also known as kimbap, is a beloved Korean dish that looks similar to sushi but has its own unique flavour and style. Where sushi rice is seasoned with vinegar, the rice for gimbap is seasoned with salt and sesame oil. Common fillings include spinach, carrot, cucumber, pickled radish, beef, ham, tuna and egg strips. Modern variations also include ingredients such as kimchi, bulgogi or cheese. The fillings are rolled up in the gim (dried seaweed) sheets, then cut into bite-sized pieces. Street stands and markets sell gimbap in neatly packed pieces that can be enjoyed without utensils, making it easy and convenient to eat on the go.

김밥

GIMBAP (SEAWEED RICE ROLLS)

- 200 g (7 oz) short-grain white rice
- 1 tablespoon sesame oil
- ¾ teaspoon salt
- 4 gim (dried seaweed) sheets
- 80 g (2¾ oz) spinach, blanched and seasoned with salt
- 300 g (10½ oz) tofu, sliced and pan-fried, seasoned with salt
- 50 g (1¾ oz) cucumber, julienned
- 50 g (1¾ oz) carrots, julienned and cooked

Combine rice and 240 ml (8 fl oz) of water in a saucepan over medium heat. Bring to the boil, then reduce heat to low and cook for about 10 minutes. Mix the rice with the sesame oil and salt. Leave to cool for a few minutes.

If you have a bamboo mat, place a gim sheet on the mat and put a thin layer of rice on the gim sheet, allowing about 5 cm (2 in) uncovered by the rice on one side. (If you don't have a bamboo mat, place the gim sheet on a kitchen board.) Place the spinach, tofu, cucumber and carrot in a neat line across the edge of the rice.

Hold the bamboo mat and the bottom edge of the gim sheet with both hands, and roll it up tightly. (If you don't have a bamboo mat, simply hold the gim sheet with both hands while rolling.) Lift one side up and fold it over the fillings, pressing gently to keep everything together. Add a little water on the blank side of the gim sheet to help seal well. Repeat with remaining gim sheets and filling.

Before cutting the rolls, dip your knife in water so the rice doesn't stick. Cut each roll into pieces about 1 cm (½ in) thick.

PREPARATION TIME
5 minutes

COOKING TIME
15 minutes

SERVES
2

Hobak jeon is thinly sliced zucchini (courgette) dipped in flour and beaten egg, which is then pan-fried until golden and crispy. The zucchini used is aehobak ('Korean zucchini' or 'grey zucchini'). Pale green in colour, it's slightly sweeter and has a thinner skin than the more common dark green zucchini.

After frying, the zucchini is sweet and tender, while the outside becomes pleasantly crisp. Many people add a thin slice of chilli to each piece of zucchini to give it an extra kick, and serve it with a soy-based dipping sauce. If you see hobak jeon at a food stall, don't miss it – freshly fried on the griddle, it's especially delicious.

호박전

HOBAK JEON (PAN-FRIED ZUCCHINI FRITTERS)

- 3 tablespoons soy sauce
- 1 tablespoon rice vinegar
- 1 teaspoon sugar
- 1 teaspoon sesame oil
- 1 teaspoon toasted sesame seeds
- 60 ml (2 fl oz/¼ cup) canola (rapeseed) oil
- 100 g (3½ oz) plain (all-purpose) wheat flour
- 200 ml (7 fl oz) sparkling water
- 2 Korean zucchini (aehobak), sliced about 8 mm (¼ in) thick
- 1 green chilli, destemmed and thinly sliced (optional)
- 1 cayenne chilli, destemmed and thinly sliced (optional)

In a bowl, mix the soy sauce, rice vinegar, sugar, sesame oil and sesame seeds.

Heat a non-stick pan over medium–high heat and, once hot, add canola oil.

Place the flour and sparkling water in separate bowls. Working in batches, coat each piece of sliced zucchini first in flour, then dip it in the sparkling water, coat again with flour, then add it to the pan. If you like, lightly press a thin slice of green chilli or cayenne chilli in the middle of each piece of zucchini.

Pan-fry zucchini slices until both sides are golden and crispy, then transfer to a serving plate and serve with the sauce.

PREPARATION TIME
1 hour

COOKING TIME
15 minutes

MAKES
6

Also known as 'hoeddeok', this a sweet pancake filled with brown sugar. At street markets, you'll see vendors wrapping the filling with the sticky dough and immediately placing it on a hot griddle. You can hear the sizzling sound and smell the sweet aroma.

The outside of the pancake becomes very crisp after frying while the sugary filling melts into a rich syrup, creating a delicious contrast. A bite into hotteok is instantly comforting, and its warmth and sweetness make it an ideal snack for cooler days. Cinnamon, peanuts and sesame can also be added to the filling.

호떡

HOTTEOK (SWEET PANCAKES WITH BROWN SUGAR)

- 300 g (10½ oz) plain (all-purpose) wheat flour
- 100 g (3½ oz) glutinous rice flour
- ¼ teaspoon salt
- 1 tablespoon sugar
- 2 teaspoons instant dried yeast
- 60 ml (2 fl oz/¼ cup) canola (rapeseed) oil, plus extra for greasing
- 100 g (3½ oz) soft brown sugar
- 2 tablespoons ground cinnamon
- 1 tablespoon toasted sesame seeds

Mix the wheat flour, glutinous rice flour and salt in a bowl. In a separate bowl, mix sugar, yeast and 300 ml (10 fl oz) of water, then pour the wet ingredients into the dry ingredients and mix everything together to form a dough. Brush the dough with a thin layer of extra oil, cover with a lid or tea towel (dish towel) and set aside for 1–2 hours, until it doubles in size.

In a bowl, mix the soft brown sugar with cinnamon and sesame seeds. Set aside.

To avoid stickiness, wear kitchen gloves greased with a little extra oil (or just put a little oil on your hands). Divide the dough into six portions. Take one portion, hold it on your palm and flatten it until it is about the size of your palm. Place a tablespoon of the brown sugar filling in the middle, then carefully press the edges of the dough together to enclose the filling. Press the dough flat again into a thick round. Repeat with the remaining dough portions. (Avoid holding the dough too long in your hand or it will get sticky.)

Heat a non-stick frying pan over low–medium heat and add the oil.

Cook each pancake for 2–3 minutes, until one side is golden and crispy, then flip and pan-fry the other side for another 2–3 minutes.

COOKING TIME
5 minutes

MAKES
1

Dalgona is a nostalgic treat made from just two ingredients. Sugar is melted until it caramelises, then bicarb is added, causing the melted sugar to magically puff up and turn golden brown. The mixture is quickly pressed flat and stamped with fun shapes like stars, circles or hearts, before it hardens into a crunchy candy.

Popular with children in the 1960s, dalgona was not only a sweet treat but a source of fun for street vendors and customers: if the customer could cut out the stamped shape without breaking it, they'd win a small prize. Dalgona gained international attention in 2021 after appearing in the TV show *Squid Game*.

50 g (1¾ oz) sugar

1 pinch (about ⅙ teaspoon) bicarbonate of soda (baking soda)

달고나

DALGONA (SUGAR CANDY)

Add sugar to a stainless-steel ladle or a small saucepan over the lowest heat.

Using a chopstick, stir for a few minutes until the sugar melts completely. Add a pinch of bicarb and immediately turn off the heat. Stir for about 10 seconds until the sugar mixture turns a light-brown caramel colour.

Pour the sugar mixture onto a non-stick surface. About 5 seconds later, press it flat with something that is completely flat and non-stick (such as the base of a stainless-steel pot).

Press your cookie cutter of choice in the sugar mixture promptly and remove it right away. Let it set for 1–2 minutes until it has hardened and cooled.

JAPAN

The history of street food in Japan dates back to the Edo period (1603–1868), when street markets first began. In the late Edo, nigiri sushi, tempura and soba became popular as quick meals and street foods. As the street food culture developed, yatai (traditional food stalls or carts) emerged, becoming widespread in the Meiji period (1868–1912). Usually open from the early evening to late at night, locals will gather around yatai after work, sharing food and drinks and chatting with each other. Yatai offer more than just tasty street food; they create a lively social atmosphere in a casual and communal setting.

In Japanese cuisine, the focus is on the quality, freshness and seasonality of the food. This also applies to the street food scene. Fresh ingredients are often seasoned lightly to bring out the natural flavours of the produce. Refreshing dishes like sōmen (cold noodles) are typically eaten in summer, while hearty stews like oden (hotpot, page 208) are more popular during colder months.

Seafood, meat, rice, and wheat-based noodles and pancakes are at the centre of Japanese street food. A series of soy sauces, miso and dashi are common in many dishes, adding depth and umami flavour.

PREPARATION TIME
2 hours

COOKING TIME
15 minutes

MAKES
24

Originating in Osaka, takoyaki is hands-down the most popular Japanese street food. To make these golden-brown balls, you'll need a takoyaki pan, available from kitchenware stores or online. The balls are usually filled with octopus, but mushrooms are a delicious substitute. Tenkasu (tempura crumbs), which can be bought in a packet, add crunch and texture.

たこ焼き

TAKOYAKI ('OCTOPUS' BALLS)

- 1 king oyster mushroom, diced into 1 cm (½ in) cubes
- 150 g (5½ oz) plain (all-purpose) wheat flour
- ½ teaspoon baking powder
- 60 ml (2 fl oz/¼ cup) canola (rapeseed) oil
- 50 g (1¾ oz) cabbage, shredded
- 2 spring onions (scallions), chopped
- 30 g (1 oz) tenkasu (tempura crumbs)
- 30 g (1 oz) beni shōga (pickled red ginger), chopped
- 60 g (2 oz) vegan mayonnaise
- 4 tablespoons aonori (dried seaweed) flakes

VEGAN DASHI

- ½ kombu sheet
- 2 dried shiitake mushrooms
- 1 spring onion (scallion), sliced
- 1 tablespoon Japanese light soy sauce
- 1 tablespoon mirin
- ½ teaspoon sugar
- pinch of salt

TAKOYAKI SAUCE

- 2 tablespoons chuno sauce
- 1 tablespoon vegan mentsuyu sauce (or ½ tablespoon soy sauce mixed with ½ tablespoon vegan dashi)
- 1 teaspoon tomato sauce (ketchup)
- 1 teaspoon sugar

To make the vegan dashi, combine the kombu, shiitake mushrooms and 300 ml (10 fl oz) of lukewarm water in a saucepan for 2 hours. Place the saucepan over medium heat and slowly bring the mixture to the boil. Just before boiling, remove the kombu. Cook the shiitake for 10 minutes, add the spring onion and cook for another 2 minutes.

Discard the shiitake and spring onion, and add the soy sauce, mirin, sugar and salt. Add the diced king oyster mushroom and cook for 1 minute, then turn off the heat and, using a slotted spoon, remove the mushroom onto a plate. Set the dashi aside to cool down.

When the dashi has cooled to lukewarm, mix it with the wheat flour and baking powder until it turns into a smooth batter.

To make the takoyaki sauce, mix the ingredients for the sauce in a small saucepan over low heat and cook for 1 minute.

Heat a takoyaki pan over medium–high heat. Brush a layer of oil over the surface of the pan and pour in the batter to fill the holes (don't worry if the batter oozes out a little).

In each hole, put 1–2 pieces of king oyster mushroom, a little bit of cabbage, spring onion, tenkasu and beni shōga. When the batter starts to cook, use a skewer to tuck any batter that has spilled outside the holes back inside. Then, turn each takoyaki 90 degrees, pour in a bit more batter to fill the hole and turn again. If there is still a gap, pour in more batter until the takoyaki become fully round.

Keep turning and frying the takoyaki for a few minutes until golden and crispy on the outside. Thread the balls onto skewers and drizzle with takoyaki sauce and vegan mayonnaise. Sprinkle with aonori flakes to serve.

PREPARATION TIME
15 minutes

COOKING TIME
10 minutes

MAKES
2

Okonomiyaki (roughly translated as 'grilled as you like') is a versatile savoury pancake. Pureed yam is often added to the batter to enhance the texture (make sure to wear kitchen gloves when you prepare the yam, as its slime can irritate the skin).

Cooked on a teppan (flat griddle), the pancake is typically topped with okonomiyaki sauce, mayonnaise, seaweed flakes, bonito flakes and sometimes beni shōga. Especially popular at food stalls during festivals, it's a tasty, comforting and filling snack that can be enjoyed on the go.

お好み焼き

OKONOMIYAKI (SAVOURY PANCAKE)

- 150 g (5½ oz) plain (all-purpose) wheat flour
- 200 g (7 oz) fresh yam, peeled and pureed
- 150 ml (5 fl oz) plant-based milk
- 2 garlic cloves, minced
- 200 g (7 oz) cabbage, shredded
- 50 g (1¾ oz) onion, diced
- 100 g (3½ oz) smoked tofu, cut into thin strips
- 1 spring onion (scallion), sliced
- ½ teaspoon salt
- ½ teaspoon ground black pepper
- 60 ml (2 fl oz/¼ cup) canola (rapeseed) oil
- 40 g (1½ oz) vegan mayonnaise
- 2 tablespoons aonori (dried seaweed) flakes
- 30 g (1 oz) beni shōga (pickled red ginger)

OKONOMIYAKI SAUCE

- 3 tablespoons chuno sauce
- 1 tablespoon vegan oyster sauce
- 1 tablespoon tomato sauce (ketchup)
- 1 teaspoon maple syrup

In a large bowl, mix the wheat flour, pureed yam and plant-based milk to form a batter. Add the garlic, cabbage, onion, smoked tofu, spring onion, salt and ground black pepper, and mix well.

To make the okonomiyaki sauce, mix the chuno sauce, vegan oyster sauce, tomato sauce and maple syrup in a small bowl.

Heat a non-stick frying pan over medium heat. Add 2 tablespoons of the canola oil and tilt the pan a little so the oil covers the base of the pan evenly. Add half of the batter and, using a spatula, press it into a flat pancake about 1 cm (½ in) thick.

Cook for 1 minute, then cover and cook for another 3–4 minutes, until lightly browned. Place a plate that's larger than the frying pan over the pan, flip the pan carefully and slide the pancake back into the pan. Cook the other side for another 2–3 minutes, until lightly browned.

Regrease the pan with the remaining canola oil and repeat to make another pancake.

Brush the sauce on the top of the okonomiyaki, squeeze over the vegan mayonnaise, and sprinkle with aonori flakes and beni shōga to serve.

PREPARATION TIME
45 minutes

COOKING TIME
15 minutes

MAKES
12

These grilled skewers are one of the best-known foods at izakaya, a type of informal bar in Japan where people socialise after work. Although yakitori means 'grilled bird' and the skewers are traditionally made with chicken, they are also made with other meats and vegetables, seasoned simply with salt or brushed with a sweet sauce. For this vegan version, I use tofu, mushrooms, leek and zucchini.

Yakitori are often found at carts and stalls known as yatai, where other types of street food are also sold. Locals and tourists alike gather around yatai in busy night markets to enjoy yakitori with a glass of sake or beer.

焼(き)鳥

YAKITORI (GRILLED SKEWERS)

- 200 ml (6¾ fl oz) Japanese all-purpose seasoning soy sauce
- 120 ml (4 fl oz) mirin
- 1 tablespoon vegan oyster sauce
- 3 tablespoons sake
- 3 tablespoons sugar
- 2 tablespoons soft brown sugar
- 80 g (2¾ oz) onion, sliced
- 100 g (3½ oz) carrots, thinly sliced
- 300 g (10½ oz) leek (white part only, choose one with a thinner stem), cut into 3 cm (1¼ in) lengths
- 9 fresh shiitake mushrooms
- 200 g (7 oz) semi-firm or firm tofu, cut into pieces 1.5 cm (½ in) thick
- 100 g (3½ oz) oyster mushrooms
- 100 g (3½ oz) zucchini (courgette), sliced 8 mm (⅓ in) thick

In a saucepan, mix the soy sauce, 75 ml (2½ fl oz) of the mirin, vegan oyster sauce, sake, sugar, soft brown sugar, onion, carrot and half the leek. Cook over low heat for 15 minutes.

Cut a cross on the cap of the shiitake mushrooms, so they can better absorb the sauce. Brush the remaining mirin on the surface of the mushroom, tofu, oyster mushrooms and zucchini and set aside to marinate for at least 30 minutes.

Push 3 shiitake mushrooms on each of 3 skewers. Push 3 pieces of tofu and 2 pieces of leek between the tofu on each of 5 skewers. Push the zucchini onto 2 skewers and the oyster mushrooms onto 2 skewers to make 12 skewers.

Preheat a chargrill to high. Brush skewers on both sides with the sauce and grill for 1–2 minutes, until half-cooked. Brush skewers with the sauce on both sides again, and continue to cook. Once the skewers are almost fully cooked, brush with the sauce for the last time and grill to finish cooking.

PREPARATION TIME
15 minutes

COOKING TIME
15 minutes

SERVES
2

Yakisoba is a Japanese fried noodle dish, traditionally made with fresh ramen noodles, pork and vegetables. It's seasoned with a tangy sauce, which gives the dish a savoury-sweet, umami-rich flavour. Yakisoba uses similar garnishes to the savoury pancake okonomiyaki (page 198).

At festivals and food markets, vendors fry the noodles with other fresh ingredients on large griddles in front of their customers, filling the air with the sound of sizzling noodles and the aroma of caramelised sauce. Often served in paper trays or bowls, yakisoba makes a delicious and satisfying snack or a quick meal.

焼きそば

YAKISOBA (STIR-FRIED NOODLES)

- 300 g (10½ oz) fresh ramen noodles
- 3 tablespoons canola (rapeseed) oil
- 60 g (2 oz) onion, thinly sliced
- 150 g (5½ oz) smoked tofu, thinly sliced
- 100 g (3½ oz) cabbage, sliced
- 1 spring onion (scallion), cut into 3 cm (1¼ in) lengths
- ½ teaspoon ground black pepper
- 3 tablespoons aonori (dried seaweed) flakes
- 30 g (1 oz) beni shōga (pickled red ginger)

YAKISOBA SAUCE

- 3 tablespoons chuno sauce
- 1 tablespoon soy sauce
- 1½ tablespoons vegan oyster sauce
- 1 tablespoon tomato sauce (ketchup)
- 2 teaspoons sugar

To make the yakisoba sauce, mix the chuno sauce, soy sauce, vegan oyster sauce, tomato sauce and sugar in a small bowl.

Cook the ramen noodles for 1 minute less than the time indicated on the packet instructions so they won't be overcooked later while stir-frying. Drain the water and coat the noodles evenly with 1 tablespoon of the canola oil so they don't stick together.

Heat a wok over medium–high heat and, once hot, add the remaining canola oil, the onion and smoked tofu. Cook, stirring, for 1–2 minutes, until the onion changes colour. Add cabbage and stir for another 1–2 minutes, until the colour of the cabbage brightens.

Increase heat to high, add the prepared noodles to the wok and mix. Add the yakisoba sauce, continuing to stir. When all the ingredients are evenly coated with the sauce, add the spring onion and ground black pepper, and stir for 30 seconds more.

To serve, top the noodles with the aonori flakes and beni shōga.

PREPARATION TIME
45 minutes

COOKING TIME
10 minutes

MAKES
8

Related to the French croquette, which was introduced to Japan during the Meiji Restoration era, korokke is both traditional and modern. It is a yōshoku dish, which refers to Western-influenced cooking brought to Japan during the same era and later 'Japanised'. Other yōshoku dishes are curry and tonkatsu (fried pork cutlet).

This common snack can be found at every supermarket, convenience store and street market. Most families also have their own way of making it at home. It's normally eaten as is, with a tonkatsu sauce, or used as a topping for noodles or as a sandwich filling.

コロッケ

KOROKKE (CROQUETTES)

- 1 tablespoon salt
- 600 g (21⅕ oz) potatoes
- 600 ml (20½ fl oz) canola (rapeseed) oil
- 120 g (4½ oz) vegan mince
- 80 g (2¾ oz) onion, finely chopped
- 1 tablespoon sugar
- 3 tablespoons soy sauce
- 100 g (3½ oz) plain (all-purpose) wheat flour
- 300 ml (10 fl oz) sparkling water
- 100 g (3½ oz) panko (Japanese) breadcrumbs

Bring a large saucepan of water to the boil, add salt and potatoes, and cook until done. (Check whether the potatoes are ready by inserting a fork into the thickest part of the potato; if it goes in smoothly, the potato is cooked.) Soak the potatoes in cold water until they are cool enough to handle, then drain, peel and mash.

Heat a non-stick frying pan over medium heat and, once hot, add 3 tablespoons of the oil and vegan mince, breaking it into small pieces with a spatula. Add the onion and cook, stirring, for 2–3 minutes until the colour changes.

Add sugar and soy sauce, then mix and add the mashed potato. Turn off the heat and mix everything together. Once the mixture is cool enough to handle, divide the mixture roughly into 8 portions and press each portion firmly into the shape of a thick patty. Set aside to rest for 15 minutes.

Set up three separate bowls; one containing the flour, one with sparkling water and the third with the panko. Coat each patty first with flour, then dip quickly in the sparkling water, then roll in the panko to coat. Press the panko firmly into the patty to ensure it is evenly coated.

Heat the remaining oil in a large saucepan over a medium–high heat. To check whether the oil is hot enough for deep-frying, hold a wooden chopstick in the oil. If it is immediately surrounded by tiny bubbles, the oil is ready to use.

Working in batches, add korokke to the oil and deep-fry for about 1–2 minutes until golden. Remove from the oil using a slotted spoon and transfer to a serving dish.

bodied, highvowelcome of consumer.
get a substantial growth.

concentrated in Europ
America, South Amer
Middle East and ha
lonial rule in As
Africa.
processed baked

PREPARATION TIME
2 hours

COOKING TIME
10 minutes

SERVES
2

Karaage is Japanese fried chicken. The bite-sized chicken is first marinated, coated in wheat flour and wheat starch, then deep-fried to crispy golden perfection. I use mushrooms for the vegan version.

This is the ultimate street food: quick, flavourful, easy to eat on the go and always available freshly fried at food stalls. It is often found at festivals, markets and outdoor events in Japan.

Serve karaage with lemon wedges or a dip such as vegan mayonnaise. If you like it spicy, sprinkle it with shichimi, a spice blend known as 'seven-flavour chilli pepper'.

から揚げ

KARAAGE (FRIED 'CHICKEN')

- 500 g (1 lb 2 oz) king oyster mushrooms, cut into chunks about 2 cm (¾ in) wide
- 10 g (¼ oz) fresh ginger, minced
- 2 garlic cloves, minced
- ½ teaspoon ground black pepper
- 60 ml (2 fl oz/¼ cup) soy sauce
- 2 tablespoons sake
- 3 tablespoons vegan mayonnaise
- 1 teaspoon salt
- 80 g (2¾ oz) wheat starch
- 150 g (5½ oz) plain (all-purpose) wheat flour
- 500 ml (17 fl oz/2 cups) canola (rapeseed) oil
- ½ lemon, cut into wedges

Mix the king oyster mushroom with the ginger, garlic, ground black pepper, soy sauce, sake, vegan mayonnaise and salt. Set aside to marinate for 2 hours.

In a bowl, mix the wheat starch and 2 tablespoons of water. Add the flour and mix everything together. Coat the mushrooms evenly with the flour mixture, pressing to make the flour mixture attach more firmly on the surface of the mushrooms.

Heat the oil in a large saucepan over medium–high heat. To check whether the oil is hot enough for deep-frying, hold a wooden chopstick in the oil. If it is immediately surrounded by tiny bubbles, the oil is ready to use.

Working in batches, add the mushrooms and deep-fry until golden. Remove from the oil using a slotted spoon and place on a serving dish with lemon wedges.

PREPARATION TIME
3 hours

COOKING TIME
40 minutes

SERVES
2

A nabemono ('things in a pot' or 'one-pot') dish, oden is a stew or soup in which thinly sliced meat and vegetables are cooked. The base is a light dashi broth flavoured with soy sauce. The combinations of ingredients you can cook in the light dashi broth are endless, but daikon (white radish) is a must!

Found not only at stalls and markets but at most convenience stores in Japan, South Korea and China, oden is slow-simmered to maximise flavour and is especially popular during winter.

Aburaage is made by deep-frying thin slices of tofu. It's commonly used in Japanese cooking to add texture to soups and stir-fries. You'll find it in Asian stores.

おでん

ODEN (HOTPOT)

- 8 fresh or dried kelp knots
- 100 g (3½ oz) fresh tofu skin (baiye tofu) sheets
- 200 g (7 oz) enoki mushrooms
- 300 g (10½ oz) daikon (white radish), sliced about 1.5 cm (½ in) thick
- 200 g (7 oz) black konjac cake
- 10 aburaage
- 10 fresh shiitake mushrooms
- 2 king oyster mushrooms, sliced about 2 cm (¾ in) thick
- 200 g (7 oz) oyster mushrooms
- 200 g (7 oz) potatoes, peeled and sliced

BROTH

- 2 kombu sheets
- 8 dried shiitake mushrooms
- 2 spring onions (scallions), sliced
- 100 ml (3½ fl oz) Japanese light soy sauce
- 100 ml (3½ fl oz) mirin
- 1 teaspoon salt
- 1 tablespoon sugar

If using dried kelp knots, first soak them for 1 hour, then drain. Cut the tofu skin sheets into strips about 5 cm x 10 cm (2 in x 4 in).

Cut about 2 cm (¾ in) off the bottom of the enoki mushrooms and separate them into small bundles. Place a bundle of the mushrooms in the middle of each sheet and wrap tightly, then push a barbecue skewer through to secure the roll. Make enough rolls to use up all the enoki mushrooms and tofu skin sheets.

To make the broth, combine the kombu sheets, dried shiitake mushrooms and 2 litres (68 fl oz) of lukewarm water in a saucepan and set aside for 2 hours.

Place the pan over medium heat. Just before boiling, remove the kombu and set it aside. Cook the shiitake for 10 minutes, add the spring onion and cook for a further 2 minutes.

Turn off the heat, discard the shiitake and spring onion. Add soy sauce, mirin, salt and sugar to the broth and mix well.

Add the kelp knots, tofu skin rolls, radish, black konjac cake, aburaage, fresh shiitake mushrooms, king oyster mushroom, oyster mushroom and potato to the broth. Bring to the boil over low–medium heat and simmer for 20 minutes before serving.

PREPARATION TIME
15 minutes

COOKING TIME
15 minutes

MAKES
10 mochi (the size of a table-tennis ball)

Since it became popular around the world in the 1990s, everyone knows mochi. A rice cake made from glutinous rice flour, mochi comes in various forms in Japan, with different fillings and coatings. Kinako mochi is a traditional dessert, made by simply coating the soft and chewy mochi with kinako, a roasted soybean flour with a nutty and slightly sweet flavour.

A delightful and not overly sweet snack that can be enjoyed at any time of the day, kinako mochi is a popular street food that is especially common in the New Year season in Japan.

きな粉餅

KINAKO MOCHI (MOCHI WITH TOASTED SOYBEAN FLOUR)

- 200 g (7 oz) glutinous rice flour
- 40 g (1½ oz) cornflour (cornstarch)
- 300 ml (10 fl oz) plant-based milk
- 100 g (3½ oz) sugar
- 100 g (3½ oz) kinako (toasted soybean flour)

Mix the glutinous rice flour, cornflour, plant-based milk and 70 g (2½ oz) of the sugar in a bowl. Strain through a sieve to remove any lumps. In a separate bowl, mix the kinako with the remaining sugar.

Pour the mixture into a non-stick saucepan over low heat and cook, stirring constantly with a silicone spatula. After a few minutes, the liquid will gradually turn into a dense paste. When all the liquid is absorbed and the mixture is completely cooked, transfer to a kitchen surface.

Wearing kitchen gloves, pull and fold the dough a few times and knead into a smooth dough.

Separate the dough into about 10 small portions (depending on how large you would like your mochi). Using your palms, shape each portion into a ball, then add to the bowl of kinako mixture, rolling the ball around until it is evenly coated.

Mochi are best when eaten fresh – they're wonderfully soft and chewy. If you need to keep them, they can be stored in an airtight container in the fridge for up to 48 hours; however, they will harden, so let them return to room temperature before serving.

PREPARATION TIME
15 minutes

COOKING TIME
10 minutes

MAKES
4

Dorayaki is perhaps best known among manga and animation lovers. It is the favourite snack of Doraemon, a time-travelling robotic cat created by Fujiko Fujio. The snack and its association with this anime character has become iconic.

A traditional sweet in Japan, dorayaki consists of two fluffy pancakes with a filling between them. The classic filling, sweetened red (adzuki) bean paste, can be found at Asian stores, but other fillings include matcha cream, custard, mochi and chocolate. At many stores and food stalls, dorayaki is freshly made and served warm.

銅鑼焼き

DORAYAKI (RED BEAN PANCAKES)

- 200 g (7 oz) wheat flour (preferably cake flour)
- 40 g (1½ oz) sugar
- ½ tablespoon baking powder
- 300 ml (10 fl oz) plant-based milk
- 100 g (3½ oz) sweetened red (adzuki) bean paste

In a bowl or jug, mix the flour, sugar, baking powder and plant-based milk to form a smooth batter.

Heat a non-stick frying pan over medium heat and, once hot, reduce heat to low. Carefully pour one-eighth of the batter into the middle of the pan so it becomes a round pancake with a diameter of about 10 cm (4 in).

Cook until big bubbles appear and pop, then lift the side of the pancake to check the base. When the base is brown, flip the pancake and let the other side cook for about 30 seconds more. Repeat to make 8 pancakes.

Spread each pancake with a layer of the red bean paste, then sandwich with another pancake. Repeat to make 4 dorayaki.

2F
T HOUSE
KOISAN DŌRI
JUPITER
LIL MOON
iPhoneX,XS
SALE
¥500
iPhoneMAX
SALE
¥500
SECRET CANDY MAGIC 1DAY

金
12 - 1
月光仮面
肉匠
焼とり

INDEX

D

F

G

H

I

N

O

P

R

S

ABOUT THE AUTHOR

Yang Liu (opposite, left) was born in Hunan province in China and spent her early years moving around the country's regions, sampling the many different cuisines. Ten years ago, she moved to Spain, where she met her partner, Katharina Pinczolits (opposite, right). The pair, who now live in Austria, became vegan and started exploring and experimenting with vegan cuisine. Their Instagram account littlericenoodle, where they post videos of how to make vegan Asian food, has more than 330,000 followers.

Published in 2026 by Hardie Grant Books, an imprint of Hardie Grant Publishing

Hardie Grant Books (Melbourne)
Wurundjeri Country
Level 11, 36 Wellington Street
Collingwood, Victoria 3066

Hardie Grant North America
2912 Telegraph Ave
Berkeley, California 94705

hardiegrant.com/books

Hardie Grant acknowledges the Traditional Owners of the Country on which we work, the Wurundjeri People of the Kulin Nation and the Gadigal People of the Eora Nation, and recognises their continuing connection to the land, waters and culture. We pay our respects to their Elders past and present.

A catalogue record for this book is available from the National Library of Australia

Vegan Asian Street Food
ISBN 978 1 76145 176 8
ISBN 9 781 76145 177 5 (ebook)

10 9 8 7 6 5 4 3 2 1

Publisher: Simon Davis
Editorial Director: Jasmin Chua
Project Editor: Nicci Dodanwela
Editor: Pru Engel
Creative Director: Kristin Thomas
Designer: George Saad
Photographer: Katharina Pinczolits
Head of Production: Todd Rechner
Production Controller: Elly Cridland

Colour reproduction by Splitting Image Colour Studio
Printed in China by Leo Paper Products Ltd.

The paper this book is printed on is from FSC® certified forests and other sources. FSC® promotes environmentally responsible, socially beneficial and economically viable management of the world's forests.